HARCOURT
TROPHIES

A HARCOURT READING/LANGUAGE ARTS PROGRAM

CHANGING PATTERNS

SENIOR AUTHORS
Isabel L. Beck ◆ Roger C. Farr ◆ Dorothy S. Strickland

AUTHORS
Alma Flor Ada ◆ Marcia Brechtel ◆ Margaret McKeown
Nancy Roser ◆ Hallie Kay Yopp

SENIOR CONSULTANT
Asa G. Hilliard III

CONSULTANTS
F. Isabel Campoy ◆ David A. Monti

 **Harcourt**

Orlando   Boston   Dallas   Chicago   San Diego

Visit *The Learning Site!*

www.harcourtschool.com

Printed in the United States of America

ISBN 0-15-322476-2

7 8 9 10 048 10 09 08 07 06 05 04

Dear Reader,

Have you ever noticed how things around you are always changing? For example, when you look up at the sky, you might see the clouds changing shape. You'll notice that people change, too, as they grow and learn more about themselves. Changing patterns of life are everywhere.

As you read **Changing Patterns,** you will meet characters who learn about themselves and others. You will also learn skills that will help you become a better reader. As your reading skills grow, you just might be surprised at how many changing patterns you begin to see.

Stop and take a look around. A world of changing patterns is waiting for you.

Sincerely,

The Authors

The Authors

Something Special!

CONTENTS

5

WHAT A TEAM!

CONTENTS

Friends to Grow With

CONTENTS

Reading
Across
Texts

Reading
Across
Texts

Reading
Across
Texts

Using Reading Strategies

A strategy is a plan for doing something well.

You probably already use some strategies as you read. For example, you may **look at the title and pictures before you begin reading** a story. You may **think about what you want to find out while reading.** Using strategies like these can help you become a better reader.

Look at the list of strategies on page 11. You will learn about and use these strategies as you read the selections in this book. As you read, look back at the list to remind yourself of the **strategies good readers use.**

- Use Decoding/ Phonics
- Make and Confirm Predictions
- Create Mental Images
- Self-Question
- Summarize

- Read Ahead
- Reread to Clarify
- Use Context to Confirm Meaning
- Use Text Structure and Format
- Adjust Reading Rate

Here are some ways to check your own comprehension:

✔ Make a copy of this list on a piece of construction paper shaped like a bookmark.

✔ Have it handy as you read.

✔ After reading, talk with a classmate about which strategies you used and why.

Something Special!

CONTENTS

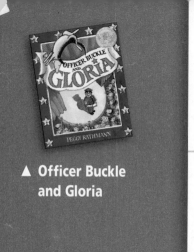

▲ Officer Buckle and Gloria

Vocabulary Power

department

noticed

audience

expression

obeys

commands

accident

"**O**fficer Buckle and Gloria" is a story about a police officer and his dog. They visit schools together to teach safety tips. Firefighters also teach us how to be safe. Look at these scrapbook pages about a visit to a fire station.

Our class learned about the people who work for our city. We found out about the work of the fire **department**. When we visited the firehouse, we **noticed** a row of beds! Firefighters live at the firehouse part of the time so they are always ready to answer a call.

A firefighter talked to us about fire safety. He made it interesting for his listeners in the **audience**. We knew from the strong **expression** in his voice that he really cared about safety.

The firefighters have a dog named Spots. When he goes with them to fires, they tell him "Sit!" and "Stay!" Spots always **obeys** their **commands**, or orders. It is important for him to follow orders. If he didn't, he might get in the firefighters' way. There could be an **accident** if someone tripped over him!

Vocabulary–Writing CONNECTION

Write three safety tips telling how to prevent an **accident** in the classroom or on the playground.

Caldecott
Medal

Fantasy

A fantasy is a story or daydream where some of the events could not happen in real life.

In this selection, look for

- events that could not really happen.

- humorous characters that may or may not be realistic.

16

OFFICER BUCKLE AND GLORIA

BY PEGGY RATHMANN

Officer Buckle knew more safety tips than anyone else in Napville. Every time he thought of a new one, he thumbtacked it to his bulletin board.

Safety Tip #77

NEVER stand on a SWIVEL CHAIR.

19

Officer Buckle shared his safety tips
with the students at Napville School.
Nobody ever listened. Sometimes,
there was snoring.

Afterward, it was business as usual. Mrs. Toppel, the principal, took down the welcome banner. "NEVER stand on a SWIVEL CHAIR," said Officer Buckle, but Mrs. Toppel didn't hear him.

Then one day, Napville's police department bought a police dog named Gloria. When it was time for Officer Buckle to give the safety speech at the school, Gloria went along.

"Children, this is Gloria," announced Officer Buckle. "Gloria obeys my commands. Gloria, SIT!" And Gloria sat.

Officer Buckle gave Safety Tip Number One:
"KEEP your SHOELACES tied!" The children
sat up and stared.

Officer Buckle checked to see if Gloria was
sitting at attention. She was.

"Safety Tip Number Two," said Officer Buckle.
"ALWAYS wipe up spills BEFORE someone
SLIPS AND FALLS!"

The children's eyes popped.

Officer Buckle checked on Gloria again.

"Good dog," he said.

Officer Buckle thought of a safety tip he had discovered that morning.

"NEVER leave a THUMBTACK where you might SIT on it!"

The audience roared.

Officer Buckle grinned. He said the rest of the tips with *plenty* of expression.

The children clapped their hands and cheered. Some of them laughed until they cried.

Officer Buckle was surprised. He had never noticed how funny safety tips could be. After this safety speech, there wasn't a single accident.

The next day, an enormous envelope arrived at the police station. It was stuffed with thank-you letters from the students at Napville School.

Every letter had a drawing of Gloria on it. Officer Buckle thought the drawings showed a lot of imagination. His favorite letter was written on a star-shaped piece of paper. It said:

You and Gloria make a good team.

Your friend,
Claire

P.S. I always wear a crash helmet.
(Safety Tip #7)

Dear Gloria and Officer Buckle,
Thanks for coming to our school.
You are nice.
Your friend,
George

#1 KEEP SHOE- LACES TIED

Officer Buckle was thumbtacking Claire's letter to his bulletin board when the phones started ringing. Grade schools, high schools, and day-care centers were calling about the safety speech.

"Officer Buckle," they said, "our students want to hear your safety tips! And please, bring along that police dog."

Officer Buckle told his safety tips to 313 schools. Everywhere he and Gloria went, children sat up and listened.

After every speech, Officer Buckle took Gloria out for ice cream. Officer Buckle loved having a buddy.

Then one day, a television news team videotaped Officer Buckle in the state-college auditorium. When he finished Safety Tip Number Ninety-nine, DO NOT GO SWIMMING DURING ELECTRICAL STORMS!, the students jumped to their feet and applauded.

"Bravo! Bravo!" they cheered.
Officer Buckle bowed again and again.

That night, Officer Buckle watched himself on the 10 o'clock news.

The next day, the principal of Napville School telephoned the police station. "Good morning, Officer Buckle! It's time for our safety speech!"

Officer Buckle frowned.

"I'm not giving any more speeches! Nobody looks at me, anyway!"

"Oh," said Mrs. Toppel. "Well! How about Gloria? Could she come?"

Someone else from the police station gave Gloria a ride to the school. Gloria sat onstage looking lonely. Then she fell asleep. So did the audience.

31

After Gloria left, Napville School had its
biggest accident ever. . . .

It started with a puddle of banana pudding. . . .
SPLAT! **SPLATTER!**

SPLOOSH! Everyone slid smack into

Mrs. Toppel,

who screamed

and let go of her hammer.

The next morning, a pile of letters arrived at the police station.

Every letter had a drawing of the accident.

Officer Buckle was shocked.

At the bottom of the pile was a note written on a paper star.

Officer Buckle smiled.

The note said:

Gloria gave Officer Buckle a big kiss on the nose. Officer Buckle gave Gloria a nice pat on the back. Then, Officer Buckle thought of his best safety tip yet . . .

Safety is very important to Peggy Rathmann. She likes to share safety information with her family and friends. It is not surprising that Officer Buckle is also very careful.

Peggy Rathmann loves dogs and other animals. Her family once had a pet dog named Skippy. He was a good dog, but sometimes he got into trouble when he thought no one was looking. The family found out about Skippy's secrets when they saw their dog on a videotape. Skippy was helping himself to breakfast from the kitchen table! Do you think that Gloria and Skippy are alike?

"Aunt Peggy is a very careful person. Not only is she careful for herself, she is careful for everyone else."

—*Robin Rathmann*
(Peggy Rathmann's niece)

Making Connections

Compare Texts

1 What special job does Officer Buckle do? What is different about the way he does it?

2 How are the two notes from Claire on pages 25 and 34 alike? How are they different?

3 Think of another funny story you know, and compare it with "Officer Buckle and Gloria." Are the stories funny in the same or different ways? Explain.

4 How do you know this story is made up?

5 How might Officer Buckle change his safety speeches from now on?

Write Home-Safety Rules

Officer Buckle talked to students about safety at school. What do you do to stay safe at home? Write a paragraph about home safety. Before you begin, make a list of five safety rules that you obey in your home. Include at least three of them in your paragraph.

Home Safety
1. (safety rule)
2. (safety rule)
3. (safety rule)
4. (safety rule)
5. (safety rule)

Writing CONNECTION

Make a Poster

To be a good citizen, Officer Buckle volunteers his time to talk to the students at Napville school. Research ways that people in your community help others. Check your public library or your newspaper for information about volunteer groups. Choose one group. Make a poster to tell people about this group and the good work they do.

Social Studies CONNECTION

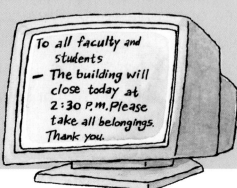

Revise an E-mail

Some words in Officer Buckle's speeches are in capital letters. Often when people send e-mail messages, they capitalize some words to show they are important. Read the message below. Then rewrite it. Capitalize the words that you think are important. Trade papers with a classmate. See if you agree.

Language Arts/Technology CONNECTION

To all faculty and students
— The building will close today at 2:30 P.M. Please take all belongings. Thank you.

Decode Long Words

Focus Skill

You know that to read a long word, you can break it into smaller parts and sound out the parts. You may notice that each part has a vowel sound. A word part with a vowel sound is called a **syllable.** Look at the chart below:

Words That Have More Than One Syllable	
Compound Words	**Words with Familiar Beginnings or Endings**
any + one = anyone police + man = policeman video + taped = videotaped	safe-ty mis-un-der-stand at-ten-tion

To decode a long word, you should first decide where each syllable ends. Here are some clues:

- When you see two or more consonants together in a word, divide the word between them. Try the short sound for the vowel in the first syllable.

$$\boxed{\text{sin}} \quad \boxed{\text{gle}}$$

- When you see one consonant between two vowels, divide the word after the first vowel. Try the long vowel sound for the first syllable. If you do not know the word, try dividing after the consonant and using the short vowel sound.

$$\boxed{\text{u}} \quad \boxed{\text{su}} \quad \boxed{\text{al}}$$

Visit *The Learning Site!*
www.harcourtschool.com

See *Skills* and *Activities*

Test Prep
Decode Long Words

▶ Read the passage. Look at the underlined words. Then answer the questions.

Dandy the Dog

Dandy is a funny little dog. When music plays, Dandy barks and dances on his back legs. When the music stops, he sits in silence. Then he runs and jumps through hoops. Dandy and his owner are very popular with children.

---

1. The first syllable in silence has—

   A the long i sound

   B the short i sound

   C the long e sound

   D the short e sound

Tip

When there is a vowel between two consonants, try pronouncing the vowel as both long and short.

2. The first syllable of popular rhymes with—

   F no

   G soap

   H hop

   J soup

Tip

If a strategy does not result in a word you know, try dividing the word a different way.

▲ Pepita Talks Twice

Vocabulary Power

languages

grumble

mumbled

darted

streak

exploded

stubborn

In the story "Pepita Talks Twice", a girl decides to make a big change. Read about a change that these animals decide to make.

All the animals spoke different **languages**. They used different words to say what they wanted to say. None of them understood what any of the others was saying.

After a while, all you could hear was a **grumble** as the animals complained in a low voice. Some of them **mumbled** and no one could hear their words clearly.

One day a bright green bird **darted**, suddenly and quickly, into the barnyard. It flew like a **streak** of light through the air, and landed on the fence. There it **exploded** in a burst of chatter, talking to all of the animals in their own languages.

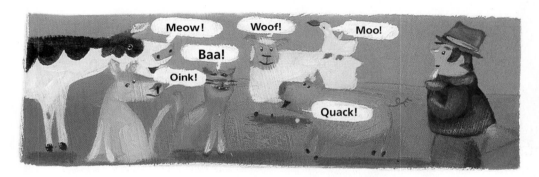

The animals saw that they had been **stubborn** about speaking only their own languages. Now they realized that if the bird could learn other languages, so could they. Once they changed their ways, the farm was never the same.

Vocabulary-Writing CONNECTION

Do you think schools should teach children to speak and write other **languages**? Write a few sentences to tell why you think as you do.

Pepita

Genre

Realistic Fiction

Realistic fiction tells about characters and events that are like people and events in real life.

In this selection, look for

- **problems that could happen in real life.**

- **a plot with a beginning, a middle, and an ending.**

44

Talks Twice

by Ofelia Dumas Lachtman

illustrated by William Low

Pepita was a little girl who spoke Spanish and English.

"Come, Pepita, please help us," people would say. Everybody called on Pepita to talk for them in Spanish and English. And she did what they asked without a grumble. Until today.

Today she didn't want to help anyone. She wanted to get home before her brother Juan (huan). She wanted to teach their dog Lobo a new trick. She wanted to teach him to fetch a ball. But if she didn't hurry, Juan would teach Lobo first.

Pepita raced by the grocery store that belonged to Mr. Hobbs, but not fast enough. "Pepita," Mr. Hobbs called. "Come speak to this lady in Spanish. Tell me what she wants!"

Pepita did what Mr. Hobbs asked. But deep inside of her a grumble began.

She tiptoed by the house where her Aunt Rosa lived, but not softly enough. "Pepita," her aunt called in Spanish. "Come talk to the delivery man in English. Tell me what he wants!"

Pepita did what Aunt Rosa asked. But deep inside of her the grumble grew.

She ducked behind the fence as she went by her neighbors' house, but not low enough.

"Pepita," Miguel (mē•gel´) called and said in Spanish, "my mother wants you to talk on the telephone in English. Please tell her what the man wants."

Pepita did what Miguel asked. But deep inside of her the grumble grew larger.

And when she went into her own yard and found her brother Juan teaching Lobo to return a ball, the grumble grew so big that it exploded.

"If I didn't speak Spanish and English," she burst out, "I would have been here first!"

49

That night as Pepita lay in bed, she thought and thought. By morning she had decided what she would do. She slipped out of bed and tiptoed by Lobo, who was sleeping on the floor. She hurried into the kitchen, where her mother was cooking breakfast and Juan was eating.

"I am never, ever going to speak Spanish anymore," Pepita said loudly.

"That's pretty dumb," Juan said.

"My, oh my, Pepita. Why?" her mother asked.

"Because I'm tired of talking twice."

"Twice?" her mother asked.

"Yes! Once in Spanish and once in English. So I'm never going to speak Spanish anymore."

Juan took a bite of tortilla and grinned. "How will you ask for enchiladas and tamales . . . and tacos with salsa?" he asked. "They are all Spanish words, you know."

"I will find a way," Pepita said with a frown. She hadn't thought about that before.

After breakfast, Pepita kissed her mother, picked up her lunch box, and started to school. Outside, she put her lunch box down and closed the gate to the fence, but not tight enough. Lobo pushed the gate open and followed at her heels.

"Wolf," Pepita scolded, "go home!" But Lobo just wagged his tail and followed her to the corner.

"Mr. Jones," Pepita said to the crossing guard, "will you please keep Wolf for me? If I take him back home, I'll be late for school."

"I'll walk him home when I'm through," Mr. Jones said. "But I thought his name was Lobo?"

"No," Pepita said. "His name is Wolf now. I don't speak Spanish anymore."

"That's too bad," said Mr. Jones, picking up his red stop sign. "I thought it was a good thing to speak two languages."

"It's not a good thing at all, Mr. Jones. Not when you have to speak twice!"

At school her teacher, Miss García, smiled and said, "We have a new student starting today. Her name is Carmen and she speaks no English. We must all be as helpful as we can."

Miss García looked at Pepita and said, "Pepita, please tell Carmen where to put her lunch and show her where everything is."

Carmen smiled at Pepita and Pepita just wanted to run away and hide. Instead, she stood up and said, "I'm sorry, Miss García, but I can't. I don't speak Spanish anymore."

"That is really too bad," her teacher said. "It's such a wonderful thing to speak two languages."

Pepita mumbled to herself, "It is not a wonderful thing at all, not when you have to speak twice!"

54

When Pepita walked into her yard after school, she found Lobo sleeping on the front porch. "Wolf, come here!" she called. "Wolf, wake up!" But he didn't open an eye or even wiggle an ear.

From the sidewalk behind her, Juan shouted, "¡Lobo! ¡Ven acá!" (bān ä•kä´) Like a streak, Lobo raced to the gate and barked.

Juan laughed and said, "Hey, Pepita, how are you going to teach old Lobo tricks if you don't speak Spanish?"

"I'll find a way," Pepita said with a frown. She had not thought about this either.

Pepita's neighbor Miguel was on the sidewalk bouncing a rubber ball. His brothers and sisters were sitting on their front porch singing. When they saw her, they called, "Come, Pepita! Sing with us!"

"I can't," she called. "All of your songs are in Spanish, and I don't speak Spanish anymore."

"Too bad," they said. "How will you help us sing at the birthday parties?"

"I'll find a way," Pepita said with a frown. This was something else she had not thought about.

At the supper table, Pepita's mother told everyone that Abuelita (ä•bwā•lē´tä), their grandmother, was coming the next day. "Abuelita says she has a new story for Pepita."

Juan laughed. "Abuelita tells all her stories in Spanish. What are you going to do now?"

"Nothing," said Pepita. "I can listen in Spanish."

"¿Qué pasa? (kā pä´sä) ¿Qué pasa?" Pepita's father said. "What is going on?"

Pepita swallowed hard. "I don't speak Spanish anymore, Papá," she said.

"Too bad," her father said. "It's a fine thing to know two languages."

"It's not a fine thing at all," Pepita said and then stopped. Her father was frowning at her.

"She even calls Lobo 'Wolf'!" Juan said.

"Wolf?" her father said, and his frown grew deeper. "Well then, Pepita, we'll have to find a new name for you, won't we? How will you answer to Pepita if that is no longer your name?"

"I'll find a way," Pepita said with a long sad sigh. This was something she had never ever thought about before.

That night when she went to bed, Pepita pulled the blankets up to her chin and made a stubborn face. "I'll find a way," she thought. "If I have to. I can call myself Pete. I can listen in Spanish. I can hum with the singing. I can call a taco a crispy, crunchy, folded-over, round corn sandwich! And Wolf will have to learn his name!" With that she turned over and went to sleep.

In the morning, when Pepita was leaving for school, her friend Miguel threw his ball into her yard. Lobo fetched it and dropped it at Pepita's feet.

"You're a good dog, Wolf," she said.

She put her lunch box down and threw the ball back to Miguel. The little boy laughed and clapped his hands. Just as she was opening the gate, he threw the ball again. This time it went into the street. Like a flash, Lobo ran after it.

"Wolf!" Pepita yelled. But Lobo didn't listen and went through the gate.

"Wolf!" Come here!" Pepita shouted. But Lobo darted right into the street.

A car was coming!

Pepita closed her eyes. "¡Lobo!" she screamed. "¡Lobo! ¡Ven acá!"

Lobo turned back just before a loud screech of the car's brakes. Pepita opened her eyes in time to see the ball roll to the other side of the street. A red-faced man shouted out the window of the car, and Lobo raced back into the yard!

Pepita shut the gate firmly behind Lobo and hugged him. "Lobo, oh, Lobo, you came when I called in Spanish!"

She nuzzled her face in his warm fur. "I'll never call you Wolf again," she said. "Your name is Lobo. Just like mine is Pepita. And, oh, Lobo, I'm glad I talked twice! It's great to speak two languages!"

Think and Respond

1 What happens when Pepita decides not to speak Spanish any more?

2 Why is this story called "Pepita Talks Twice"?

3 Why do you think Lobo doesn't listen when Pepita speaks to him in English?

4 Do you agree that Pepita is lucky to speak two **languages?** Why or why not?

5 Give an example of a reading strategy that you used while reading this story. How was it helpful?

Meet the Author
OFELIA DUMAS LACHTMAN

Ofelia Dumas Lachtman speaks both Spanish and English. She was born in the United States, but her parents and other family members were born in Mexico. As a girl, Ofelia watched American movies with her mother. She translated the words into Spanish so that her mother could understand them.

Ofelia Dumas Lachtman became a published author at the age of twelve, when her work appeared in a book of poetry. Since then she has gone on to write her own books for children and adults. Today she lives in Los Angeles, California, where she enjoys walking, listening to music, and taking care of her cats.

Making Connections

Compare Texts

1 How does Pepita learn that she has a valuable gift?

2 What do the other characters think about Pepita's ability to speak two languages? How do you know?

3 Why is it difficult for a person to change something about himself or herself? What story characters do you know who make these kinds of changes?

4 Do the characters and events in this story seem real to you? Why or why not?

5 What do you think Pepita will do the next time someone asks her to talk for them in Spanish and in English?

Write a Letter

Pepita's friends and neighbors will be happy to know that she is speaking Spanish again. Write a letter that Pepita might send to let everyone know the good news. Use a form like this one to plan your letter.

Writing CONNECTION

address
city, state
date

Dear _____
(message) _____
_____
Sincerely

name
address
city, state zip code

Make a Chart

In "Pepita Talks Twice," Pepita has many chances to help her neighbors and classmates. Go back to the story to find people who needed her help. Record the information in a chart. Use your chart to write sentences that tell why Pepita is a good person in her neighborhood.

who needs help	how she helps them

Share a Song

Pepita's friends ask her to sing Spanish songs with them. Think of a song from your culture or one that has special meaning for you. Share your song by teaching it to classmates so you can sing it together.

Narrative Elements

Like all fiction stories, "Pepita Talks Twice" has three important elements, or parts. The **setting** is the time and place in which the story is set. The **characters** are the people and animals you meet in the story. The **plot** is what happens in the story. This picture shows the three main elements of "Pepita Talks Twice."

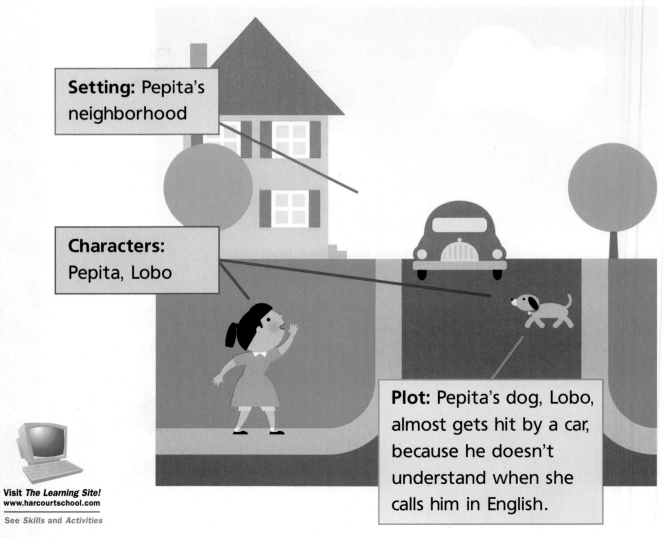

Setting: Pepita's neighborhood

Characters: Pepita, Lobo

Plot: Pepita's dog, Lobo, almost gets hit by a car, because he doesn't understand when she calls him in English.

Visit *The Learning Site!*
www.harcourtschool.com

See *Skills* and *Activities*

Test Prep
Narrative Elements

▶ **Read the story.**

Jake's Secret Cake

One day Jake invented a great new cake and called it "Jake's Secret Cake." Everyone who tried the cake wanted one. He had to bake a cake for his grandma, a cake for Parents' Night at school, and a cake for his Aunt Selma.

"I'm getting tired of baking all these cakes!" cried Jake.

The next day, the kitchen was full of people. They all watched while Jake baked his secret cake. "It's not called Jake's Secret Cake any more," he told them. "Now it's Jake's Sharing Cake!"

Now answer numbers 1 and 2. Base your answers on the story "Jake's Secret Cake."

1. Who is the main character?

   A Aunt Selma

   B Ted

   C Jake

   D Jake's grandma

Tip

Remember that the main character is the one the story is mostly about.

2. How do you know where Jake spends most of his time?

Tip

To identify the setting of a story, think about where and when the story takes place.

Vocabulary Power

specific

returned

detective

definitely

assistant

positive

case

How do you feel when you lose something that is special to you? Sometimes it helps to have another person join in the search for a lost object.

JEN: What's the matter, Jon?

JON: I lost my bottle cap.

JEN: That doesn't sound so bad.

JON: Oh, it's not an ordinary bottle cap.

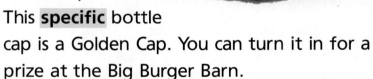

This **specific** bottle cap is a Golden Cap. You can turn it in for a prize at the Big Burger Barn.

JEN: Why don't you ask your mother about it?

JON: I can't. She isn't home. She went to the mall. The zipper on my new jeans broke.

JEN: Wait a minute. You wore the jeans?

JON: Yes, of course. How else would the zipper have broken?

JEN: And your mother has already **returned** the jeans? Has she taken them back to the store?

JON: Yes. I think I might have to hire a **detective** — you know, someone who solves mysteries.

JEN: I'm no detective, but I **definitely** know what
happened to your Golden Cap. There's no question.
JON: You do?

(Later, at the store)
WOMAN: The manager isn't
here, but I'm her **assistant**.
I help the manager with
her work. How can I
help you?
JEN: My friend Jon's mother
returned his jeans a little
while ago. I'm sure he left
something in the pocket.
In fact, I'm **positive** he
did. Can you check?

JEN: There you are, Jon. You had a problem that needed to be
solved, and I took your **case**.
JON: Yes, Jen, you solved The Case of the Missing Bottle Cap.
Now let's go to the Big Burger Barn and find out what we won!

Vocabulary–Writing CONNECTION

What kind of work does a
detective do? Would it be boring
or exciting? Write several sentences
that tell your opinion.

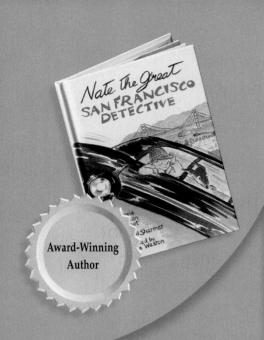

Award-Winning
Author

Mystery

A mystery is a story about something that is not known, understood, or explained.

In this selection, look for

- characters and events that are realistic.

- a problem that the main character has to solve that involves a possible crime.

Nate the Great
SAN FRANCISCO
DETECTIVE

by Marjorie Weinman Sharmat
and Mitchell Sharmat

illustrated by
Martha Weston

CHAPTER 1

MR. GREAT

My name is Nate the Great. I am a detective. My dog, Sludge, is a detective too.

This morning Sludge and I were at the airport in San Francisco. We were supposed to meet another detective there at ten o'clock. My cousin, Olivia Sharp.

Olivia always wears a boa made of feathers. This makes her easy to find. Anywhere. But all we saw were strangers. And many people with signs.

All at once, I, Nate the Great, saw a sign that said NATE THE GREAT in big letters. A man in uniform was holding it. He came up to us.

"Mr. Great and Sludge?" he said. "I'm Willie. Miss Olivia's chauffeur. She's out on her eight o'clock case. It's running late. She hasn't even started her nine o'clock." Willie picked up my suitcase. "Your limo is over there," he said.

"My limo?"

"Yes. Miss Olivia always travels in a limo. But today she saved it for you."

I, Nate the Great, had never been in a limo. Sludge had never been in a limo. It was long and shiny. We got inside. Willie got in the front seat. And we were off.

CHAPTER 2

CALLING NATE THE GREAT

We drove up and down many hills. "Is everything all right back there, Mr. Great?" Willie asked. I looked at Sludge. He wagged his tail.

"Fine," I said. "But can you tell me about the case that's making Olivia late?"

"Her friend Duncan lost a joke book," Willie said. "Miss Olivia is looking for it."

Willie drove us to Olivia's house and let us in. A telephone was ringing. And ringing. This was a phone that needed to be answered.

"Nate the Great for Olivia Sharp," I said.

"Hello, Nate." It was Annie, from back home.

"We all miss you," she said. "And Fang has something to tell you."

I heard heavy breathing. I knew that Annie's dog, Fang, was on the line. I was happy to be many miles away from his teeth. I waited. Fang had nothing else to say. Then I heard a strange voice. It belonged to Rosamond.

"My turn. Bring back California fish for my cats. Lots of fish. All the fish you can carry. Over and out."

"I thank all of you for the call," I said. Then I heard another voice.

"Wait! It's me, Claude. I lost something." Claude was always losing something.

"I lost an itsy bitsy seashell two years ago on the Golden Gate Bridge. Find it!"
Claude hung up.

CHAPTER 3

THE END OF THE WORLD

The telephone rang again. "Nate the Great for Olivia Sharp," I said.

"Hello. This is Duncan. It's eleven o'clock and the world is coming to an end." I, Nate the Great, hoped that this Duncan person did not have his information straight.

"I need Olivia," Duncan said.

"Olivia is out," I said. Duncan moaned.

"Then the world is really coming to an end."

"Could you be more specific?" I asked.

"Well," said Duncan, "I lost my joke book. I have to tell a joke to a friend at two o'clock and I forgot how it ends."

"Olivia is on your case," I said.

"Yes, I'm her case number twenty-two," Duncan said. "But she is also working on cases number eighteen and number twenty-one at the same time. She'll never solve mine by two o'clock." I, Nate the Great, had never heard such a sad voice.

"Very well," I said. "I will also take your case." I hung up.

Then I called my mother. The answering machine came on. I said,

"Dear Mother,
Sludge and I are on
a California case.
But it has something
to do with
the entire world.
Or the end of it.
Something like that.
I will be back.
Love,
Nate the Great."

CHAPTER 4

JOKE STEW

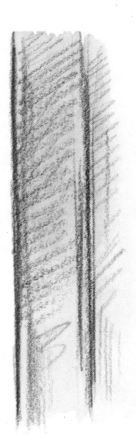

Willie drove Sludge and me to Duncan's house. "I
will wait in the limo," Willie said.

I knocked on Duncan's door. He answered it.
Duncan looked even sadder than he sounded. His hair
was hanging limp, his socks were drooping, and his
jeans were slipping. Sludge and I walked inside.

"I am Nate the Great," I said. "And this is my
assistant, Sludge. Tell us about your joke book."

"Well, I was in Booksie's Bookstore yesterday,"
Duncan said. "I saw this small book called *Joke Stew*.
It was the only copy there. I bought it. I left the
bookstore with the book in a Booksie's bag."

"Then what did you do?"

"I went to lots of other stores and bought things.
Then I went to Perry's Pancake House."

"A *pancake* house? Good thinking."

"Yes, Perry's Pancake House has this big, big menu
with five pages of different kinds of pancakes.
I started to read the menu. The waiter came by.
I ordered mushyberry pancakes. The waiter left. I kept
reading the menu. Then I took out my joke book to
find the perfect joke to tell today. I found it."

"Then what happened?"

"The waiter brought the pancakes."

"Did you put the joke book back in its bag?"

"I don't remember," Duncan said. "Because something bad happened."

"What happened?" I asked.

Duncan looked down at his feet. "I can't tell you."

"What *can* you tell me?"

"The world is coming to an end."

I, Nate the Great, wished this case were coming to an end. I said, "So the last place you saw your joke book was in the pancake house?"

"Yes."

"It might still be there," I said. I, Nate the Great, was sure of one thing. Pancakes were still there. Five pages of pancakes to choose from!

"I will be back," I said.

CHAPTER 5

STICKY, ICKY MESS

Willie drove Sludge and me to Perry's Pancake House.

"Sniff around outside, Sludge," I said. "Look for the joke book."

"I'll help Sludge," Willie said.

I went inside the pancake house. It looked good, and it smelled good. I walked up to a waiter.

"I am looking for a small joke book titled *Joke Stew*," I said.

The waiter looked mad. "A girl was just here looking for it," he said. "She was wrapped in feathers. Said she was a detective. She put up LOST JOKE BOOK signs everywhere. Here. There. Up and down the street. But we have no joke book.

"I know who lost it. Yesterday this boy came in. I served him mushyberry pancakes. He knocked the syrup bottle over everything. The pancakes, the menu, the table. Ugh! I scooped up all the sticky stuff and dumped it in a bag. I handed the bag to him. I told him that somewhere out there a hungry family of ants or flies would love this sticky, icky mess."

The waiter was getting madder. I, Nate the Great, knew that I had to leave the pancake house without eating. I did not want to do that. But I went outside. Sludge and Willie were standing there.

"We didn't find the joke book," Willie said.

"We looked in front. Then Sludge went out back. He found garbage cans. He looked in them. Isn't that the wrong place to look for a joke book?"

"Well, a good detective knows that sometimes the wrong place is the right place," I said.

"Smart dog," Willie said. Willie, Sludge, and I got into the limo.

CHAPTER 6

THE GOLDEN GATE CLUE

I liked this limo. It was a good place to think and to drive around to see San Francisco.

I, Nate the Great, was thinking. I was not having any luck with Duncan's case. I had not found his joke book. I had not found Claude's seashell either. Perhaps that was because I had not looked for it.

"To the Golden Gate Bridge, please," I said to Willie.

"A fine bridge, Mr. Great," Willie said.

When we got there, Sludge and I peered out the window. The Golden Gate Bridge was very, very big. Claude's seashell was very, very small. This was not going to help Claude. But suddenly I, Nate the Great, knew that it might help Duncan!

"I have a Golden Gate clue," I said to Willie. "Onward to Duncan's house!"

CHAPTER 7

FROZEN PANCAKES!

Duncan was waiting for us.

"I know all about the spilled syrup," I said. "What did you do with the bag the waiter gave you?"

"I put it in the freezer," Duncan said. "I like frozen pancakes."

"Did you open the bag first?"

"No, it was too icky and sticky."

I put my hand on Duncan's shoulder. "I, Nate the Great, know where your joke book is. It is in your freezer!"

"Oh, cool!" Duncan said.

Was that a joke? Never mind. "I, Nate the Great, say you were reading the menu. But you were also reading your joke book. The menu was big. The book was small. So the book must have slid or fallen into the pages of the menu. Before or while the syrup spilled. The waiter scooped everything up fast and put it all in a take-out bag."

"You are a good detective," Duncan said. "Even if you don't put up signs."

"No problem," I said. "Olivia has her way. I have mine."

I opened the freezer. I saw the bag. I took it out. I opened it. It was full of cold, crusty, icky things. Pancakes, napkins, the top from a syrup container, a little tub of butter, a huge menu . . . *but no joke book!*

"The joke book isn't here," I said. "The world is definitely coming to an end, correct?"

Duncan looked down at his feet. "Correct," he said. "I need my book at two o'clock. And it's after twelve now."

"Do not lose hope," I said. "That is the worst thing to lose."

I sat down. "I, Nate the Great, need pancakes. Sludge needs a bone. They help us think."

"Have a frozen pancake," Duncan said.

"Thaw it," I said.

"I don't thaw," Duncan said.

"Very well," I said. "A frozen pancake is better than no pancake at all. But give Sludge a nice bone."

CHAPTER 8

LOST IN THE BIG CITY

I ate a frozen mushyberry pancake. It did not help me think. Except about my cold teeth. "What happened after you left the pancake house?" I asked.

"Well, I had lots of bags. I dropped them outside the pancake house. Then I picked them up and brought them home. I put the pancake bag in the freezer and the other bags over there in that corner. But the Booksie's bag isn't there."

"Hmmm," I said.

I went over to the corner and looked inside all the bags. No book. "Both the book *and* the Booksie's bag are missing," I said. "I, Nate the Great, say that we should go to Booksie's Bookstore. I think you dropped your book in its bag when you were in front of the pancake house. It wasn't there today. Perhaps somebody found it and took it back to the store."

Duncan kept looking at his feet. "Somebody could have found it and taken it home," he said. "Or taken it on a trip. Or mailed it. Or kicked it. Anything! This is a big city. My joke book could be anywhere!"

"You are right," I said.

"I *am?*"

"Yes. This is a big-city case. Your book *could* be anywhere. But we don't have enough time to look everywhere. So I, Nate the Great, have to *choose* where to look. And because the book was probably in the Booksie's bag when you lost it, I choose Booksie's Bookstore."

"Oh," Duncan said. "There is more to this detective business than I thought."

CHAPTER 9

WHAT'S WRONG IS RIGHT

Willie drove Duncan, Sludge, and me to Booksie's Bookstore. He waited outside with Sludge. Duncan and I went inside.

"Are books returned here?" I asked a lady behind the counter.

"Yes."

"Was a joke book returned today or yesterday?"

"You're the second person to ask," the lady said. "A girl with a feather boa and a bunch of signs was just asking the same question. I told her a mystery book had been returned. And a children's book, a cookbook, and a science book. But no joke book."

"What happens when a book is brought back?" I asked.

"We put it on the shelf again," she said.

Duncan and I walked away. "Show me the joke book department," I said.

"Why? It won't be there," Duncan said.

"We can't be positive," I said.

Duncan led the way. "Here," Duncan said. "This is the exact place I found the book."

I looked around. I looked hard. The book *wasn't* there.

"You did not choose the right place in the city to look," Duncan said. I, Nate the Great, already knew that.

I saw Sludge peering through the front window. Sludge had not been much help on this case. Or had he? He had looked in the wrong place for the joke book. But he knew that sometimes the wrong place is the right place. The wrong place!

"Follow me," I said to Duncan. I rushed up and down aisles. At last I came to the place I was looking for. *The wrong place.*

I waved to Sludge. He wagged his tail. Then I looked up and down and across shelves. And there it was! Duncan's joke book. *Joke Stew!!!* I took it down and handed it to Duncan.

"My book! My book!" he said. "But this is the cookbook section. Why is my book *here?*"

"I, Nate the Great, say that the lady told us a cookbook had been returned. Whoever put your book back on the shelf thought it was a cookbook. With a name like *Joke Stew*, it could be."

Duncan smiled. He *smiled*. I knew the world was safe for now.

CHAPTER 10

A FEATHERY HUG

Duncan skipped off.

Suddenly I heard a voice. *"You solved my case number twenty-two!"*

A bunch of feathers hugged me. It was Olivia. In person. "I owe you one," she said. "Let me know if I can ever solve a case for you. Any case. Big, small, easy, hard."

"I think I have something for you right now," I said. "It's big and it's small and possibly it's hopeless. Willie can take us to it." I, Nate the Great, enjoyed the ride back to the Golden Gate Bridge.

Think and Respond

1. What does Nate do differently from Olivia to solve this **case**?

2. Why did the woman in the bookstore think the joke book was a cookbook?

3. How does Sludge help Nate solve the **case**?

4. Do you think Nate is a great detective? Why or why not?

5. How did you use a reading strategy to understand the story? Give an example.

MEET THE AUTHORS
Marjorie and Mitchell Sharmat

Marjorie Sharmat says that she gets ideas for her books from real life. Nate the Great, her favorite character, is named after her father, Nathan Weinman. Years ago, one of her sons asked her to help him rescue a skunk from a sewer. This project gave her the idea for *Nate the Great Goes Undercover.*

Marjorie Sharmat and her husband, Mitchell Sharmat, work together on many projects. They take turns suggesting ideas and lines. Mitchell Sharmat has written several books with his wife.

MEET THE ILLUSTRATOR
Martha Weston

One of Martha Weston's first jobs was as an animator. In the past, animators drew characters for cartoons and films by hand. Today a lot of animation is done with computers.

Martha Weston would rather read a book with no pictures than one with bad pictures. She believes that an illustrator should be true to the writer's words.

95

Making Connections

Compare Texts

1 What talent earns Nate the nickname Nate the Great?

2 How do Duncan's feelings change from the beginning of the story to the end? How does the author show this change?

3 Both Pepita and Nate the Great have special talents. How are Nate's feelings about his talent different from Pepita's feelings about her talent?

4 How is this mystery story different from other fiction stories you have read?

5 Do you think Nate the Great will find Claude's seashell on the Golden Gate Bridge? Explain your answer.

Write a Paragraph

Everyone loses something at one time or another. Tell about a time you lost something. What did you do to find it? What clues did you follow? Use a diagram to show the order you used as you looked for it. Then write a paragraph to describe your search.

Lost Article

First looked in:

↓

Then looked:

↓

Finally found it? Where?

Writing CONNECTION

Make a Table to Compare Bridges

Math CONNECTION

Nate the Great asks Willie to take him to the Golden Gate Bridge. Do some research to find information on the five longest suspension bridges in the United States. Make a table to show the lengths of the bridges in order from the longest to the shortest.

Plan an Experiment

Science CONNECTION

Like detectives, scientists ask a question and then think of a way to find an answer to it. How could Nate find out how cold it has to be for pancake syrup to freeze? Does it freeze as quickly as water does? Plan an experiment for Nate that could answer those questions. List the things Nate would need and the steps he would follow. Make a prediction about what he might find out.

▲ Nate the Great, San
Francisco Detective

Decode Long Words

You know that you can sometimes figure out long words by dividing them into syllables. You can also use letter patterns and spelling patterns.

- Look for letter patterns that you have seen in other words. Try the same sounds in the new word.

- Look for spelling patterns you know, such as consonant-vowel-consonant or consonant-vowel-consonant-e. Try the vowel sound you have learned for that pattern.

- Blend the sounds to say a word that makes sense.

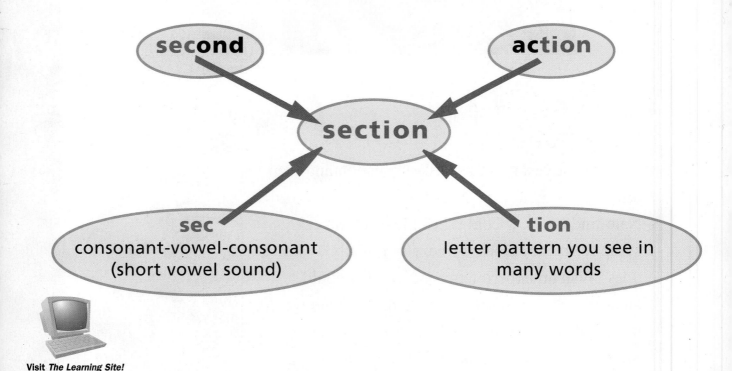

second

action

section

sec
consonant-vowel-consonant
(short vowel sound)

tion
letter pattern you see in
many words

Visit *The Learning Site!*
www.harcourtschool.com

See Skills and Activities

Test Prep
Decode Long Words

▶ **Read the passage. Look at the underlined words. Then answer the questions.**

The Case of the Missing Seeds

Mrs. Bell asked Ellie to help her solve a mystery. "I was going to plant some <u>pumpkin</u> seeds in my garden," she said. "I opened the packet and put the seeds on a little table in the yard, but now they're gone!"

Ellie was glad to help. Near the table, she found some small footprints. They led to the base of a tall tree. Ellie looked up and saw a squirrel <u>scramble</u> up onto a branch, munching away.

---

1. The vowels in <u>pumpkin</u> have—

   A one long and one short sound

   B the same vowel sound

   C long vowel sounds

   D short vowel sounds

Tip

In a consonant-vowel-consonant pattern, listen for the short sound for the vowel.

2. One part of <u>scramble</u> has a letter pattern like part of—

   F table

   G squirrel

   H scare

   J same

Tip

Look for word parts that you have seen in other words.

Vocabulary Power

aimed

pretended

familiar

captain

monitor

professional

Learning to do something new can be fun, but it isn't always easy. Read what Greg wrote about learning to build a birdhouse.

Today Grandma showed me how to build a birdhouse. First we cut out the pieces of wood. Then we nailed them together. The hardest part was driving the nails in with a hammer. I **aimed** the hammer at the nail, but I missed again and again.

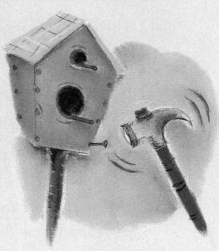

I never thought it would be so hard to strike a tiny nail with a big, heavy hammer. I **pretended** I didn't care, but it doesn't do any good to make believe with Grandma. As soon as I noticed a twinkle in her eye, I could tell what she was thinking.

"Don't give up. Try harder." That saying is **familiar** to me because Grandma says it all the time. That's why I know it so well.

Grandma helped me by showing me how it is done. She was the **captain**, and I was following her orders. Soon I had built a beautiful birdhouse. When Mom and Dad and Jimmy saw it, they applauded. Yes, even my brother Jimmy clapped!

Building things is fun. But young people should not try to do it alone. It is important to have an older **monitor** to help and watch out for things that could be dangerous. Maybe I'll be a **professional** builder someday. That would be a great job!

**Vocabulary-Writing
CONNECTION**

Write about a **familiar** saying you know or you've heard. Tell what you think it means and why you remember it.

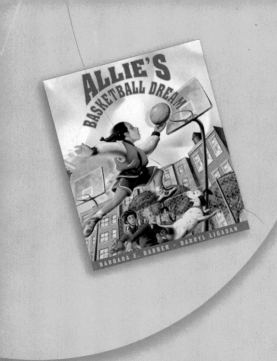

Realistic Fiction

Realistic fiction tells about characters and events that are like people and events in real life.

In this selection, look for

- a problem that could happen in real life.

- characters who have feelings that real people could have.

ALLIE'S

Basketball
Dream

by Barbara E. Barber
illustrated by Darryl Ligasan

When Allie's father came home from work
Friday evening, he brought her a gift. "Because I love
you," he said, and kissed Allie on her nose. The gift
was something that Allie really wanted—a basketball.

The next day, Allie and her father walked to the playground. Allie loved the sound her new basketball made as she bounced it on the sidewalk. As they passed the firehouse, they waved to Mr. Puchinsky, the fire captain.

"Hi, Domino!" Allie called to the firehouse dog. Domino wagged his tail and licked Allie's basketball when she held it for him to sniff.

At the playground, Allie scanned the basketball courts while her father talked with Mr. Gonzalez, the park monitor. Some older kids already had a game going. All of the players were boys. They hardly ever missed a shot.

"Go ahead and practice, and then we'll shoot baskets together as soon as I get back from taking Aunt Harriet shopping," Allie's father told her. "I'll just be across the street. If you need me, tell Mr. Gonzalez, and he'll come get me."

"Okay," Allie replied.

She waved good-bye and ran to an empty court.
She lifted her new basketball over her head and aimed.
The shot missed. She aimed again. She missed again.

One of the boys playing in the next court noticed
Allie and started to laugh. The others joined in.

"*Boys*," Allie mumbled. Then she dribbled and
bounced. And bounced and dribbled.

Allie's friend Keisha came into the playground with her hula hoop. Keisha saw Allie and held the hoop up. Allie aimed her basketball and . . . *Zoom!* Right through the middle.

"Let's play basketball!" Allie said.

"I don't know how," Keisha answered.

"I'll show you."

Keisha twirled her hula hoop. "My brother says basketball's a boy's game."

"Your brother doesn't know what he's talking about," Allie said.

She aimed at an empty trash can. She stepped back a few feet, and took a shot.

Thump! In!

Allie noticed her neighbor Buddy jumping rope with her friend Sheba and another girl. When he missed he ran off to join some other kids who wanted to use his volleyball.

"Hi, Allie!" Sheba called. "Is that your basketball?"

"Yep, my dad gave it to me. Want to shoot some baskets?"

"Maybe later," Sheba replied. "Want to jump double-dutch?"

"Maybe later," Allie said.

Allie pretended she was playing soccer. She kicked the ball and chased it. Then she looked up at the basket, aimed, and shot. The ball struck the backboard, then the rim, and bounded off.

Julio, who was in Allie's class at school, whizzed by on his skateboard. He made a sharp turn when he noticed the new basketball.

"Wow!" Julio exclaimed. "Is that yours?"

"Yes," said Allie proudly. "Let's shoot some baskets!"

Julio looked at Allie, his eyes wide. "You must be kidding!" he said. "Me shoot baskets with a girl? No, thanks!" He laughed and skated away.

Allie heaved a sigh and eyed the basket. She took another shot. The ball circled the rim and fell off. She heard some of the boys in the next court chuckle. She tried again. And again.

Allie sighed again and plopped down on a bench. Buddy walked over, bouncing his volleyball. "What's up?" he asked. "Something wrong with your basketball?"

"Well . . ." Allie hesitated.

"I'll trade you my volleyball for it! It's smaller and lighter—it'll be easier for you to play with."

"I don't know," Allie said.

Buddy reached into his pocket. He took out a miniature sports car, two quarters, and some grape bubble gum—Allie's favorite. "You can have these *and* my volleyball for the basketball," he said.

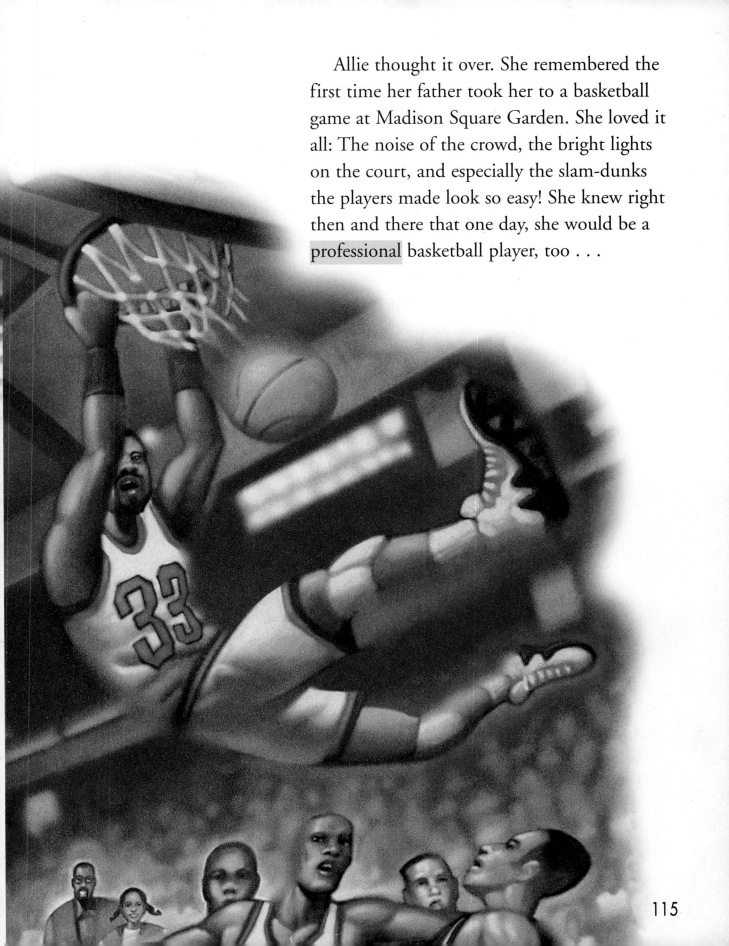

Allie thought it over. She remembered the first time her father took her to a basketball game at Madison Square Garden. She loved it all: The noise of the crowd, the bright lights on the court, and especially the slam-dunks the players made look so easy! She knew right then and there that one day, she would be a professional basketball player, too . . .

Allie hugged her basketball close. "No way I'm getting rid of this ball! It's a gift from my dad. Someday I'm going to be the best basketball player ever!"

"Well," Buddy snorted, "some guys think girls shouldn't be playin' basketball."

"That's dumb!" Allie bounced her ball. "My cousin Gwen plays on one of the best high school teams in her state. She's won more than ten trophies!"

Buddy looked surprised.

"Some girls think boys shouldn't be jumping rope," Allie continued. "They think boys are no good at it. That's dumb, too."

Buddy unwrapped two pieces of gum. "Want some?"

Allie and Buddy blew huge purple bubbles. They popped their gum so loud that Domino ran over to investigate. He pranced right up to Allie and sniffed her basketball.

"Wanna play basketball, Domino? Come on, boy, let's play!"

Domino ran alongside Allie as she dribbled and bounced. Laughing, Allie turned toward the basket, and took a long-distance shot. The ball brushed against the backboard, rolled around the rim, and dropped in!

Buddy jumped up from the bench. "Nice shot, Allie!" he yelled, and ran to retrieve the ball.

"Thanks," Allie said, beaming.

Julio saw the shot, too. So did Sheba. They both hurried to the center of the court.

"Here!" Allie and Julio and Sheba called to Buddy almost in one voice.

Buddy dribbled the ball, then passed it to Allie. She took a shot and missed.

"Don't worry, Allie!" Buddy yelled. Julio and Sheba each shot and missed. Allie caught the ball and dribbled closer to the basket. *I can't wait to show Dad what I can do,* she thought.

Up, up went the ball. It didn't touch the backboard. It didn't touch the rim. It didn't touch anything.

Zoom! In!

The older boys in the next court applauded. Mr. Gonzalez whistled. Domino barked. Above all the noise rose a familiar voice—Allie's father.

"That-a-girl!" he shouted. "Hooray for Allie!"

Think and Respond

1. What does Allie learn about playing basketball?

2. How have the attitudes of the boys on the playground changed by the end of the story?

3. What kind of **professional** basketball player would Allie be? How can you tell?

4. Do you think it is important to have a dream, as Allie does? Why or why not?

5. How did using reading strategies help you understand the story?

MEET THE AUTHOR
Barbara E. Barber

Dear Readers,

I have always loved to write. My mother says I've been writing since the second grade. I enjoy writing poetry as well as stories. My friends and family thought I should send my writing to publishers, and so I did.

Allie's Basketball Dream is my second picture book to be published. Allie's story comes from my own childhood. I liked to play basketball, punchball, and touch football. Just like Allie, I learned that practice makes perfect.

It takes time to become good at a sport. Be patient with yourself. Remember, you can do it if you try!

Your friend,

Barbara E. Barber

MEET THE ILLUSTRATOR
Darryl Ligasan

Dear Readers,

I am an illustrator. I draw and paint pictures that help an author tell a story. For *Allie's Basketball Dream,* I tried something new. These pictures were made on a computer!

First I used a pencil to draw sketches on paper. Then I used a special tool called a scanner, which took pictures of the sketches and put them into the computer. Instead of using paints and a brush, I used the computer to add details and colors to the sketches. Did you notice that parts of some pictures seem stretched? I had the computer do that for me, too!

Your friend,

Darryl Ligasan

Visit *The Learning Site!* www.harcourtschool.com

A GUIDE TO BASKETBALL

by Tina Brigham

James Naismith took a round ball and a basket and created an international pastime.

Who Started It?

In 1891, the game of basketball was invented by a young American named James Naismith. James lived in Springfield, Massachusetts, where the winter months are cold and snowy. He wanted a game he could play indoors during the cold weather.

First, he hung wooden baskets on the opposite walls of a gymnasium. Then he formed two teams. Each team tried to score points by throwing a ball into one of the baskets. Today the basket is a metal hoop and a net, and the game has become a sport played all over the world!

Tip off! The referee tosses the ball in the air to start the game. Players jump and try to tip the ball towards their teammates.

Like many sports, basketball has some special words. This glossary gives the meanings of some of those words. Use the glossary to help you read the next two pages.

Glossary of Basketball Words

defense [dē′ fens] *n.* the team that does not have the ball in play

dribble [drib′əl] *v.* to bounce the ball with one hand

foul [foul] *n.* an action that breaks the rules of a game, such as bumping or holding a player on the opposite team

goal [gōl] *n.* the basket that each team aims for with the ball

offense [ô′fens] *n.* the team that has the ball in play

quarter [kwor′tər] n. a period of play that lasts six or twelve minutes

shoot [sho̅o̅t] *v.* to throw the ball, aiming it into the basket

How the Game Is Played

In basketball, two teams compete to make the most goals. Each team has five players on the court at a time. These players are either the **offense** or the **defense**, depending on which team has the ball in play.

The game begins with a tip-off. The ball is thrown into the air, and one player from each team tries to tip the ball toward another player on his or her team. The person who gets the ball must **dribble** it to the basket and **shoot** for points.

Games are usually played in four **quarters**. The players rest after the second quarter. This break is called half-time. During the game, a scoreboard helps the players and spectators keep track of the time and the score.

Basketball is scored in different ways. Two points are usually scored for each basket. Three points are given for a basket that is made from behind a line that is 23 feet 9 inches from the basket. Three-point throws can be made at any time during the game.

Diagram of a Basketball Court

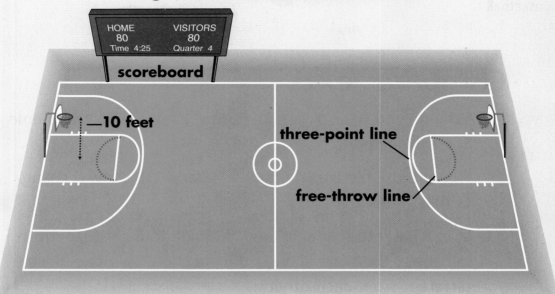

When a **foul** occurs, the person who has the ball can shoot for extra points from the free-throw line. The free-throw line is only 15 feet from the basket. All regular play is stopped during a free throw. The other players are not allowed to move around the court until the ball is in the air.

The team with the most points at the end of the fourth quarter wins the game!

Think and Respond

What part of this article best helped you understand the game of basketball? Explain your answer.

Making Connections

Compare Texts

1. Why do you think "Allie's Basketball Dream" is in the theme Something Special?

2. How do the pictures on pages 114 and 118 show a change in Allie's feelings?

3. "Allie's Basketball Dream" and "A Guide to Basketball" both tell about the same sport. How are these two selections different from each other?

4. If you didn't know this story was fiction, would you believe that it could be true? Why or why not?

5. If you wanted to learn more about basketball, how could you do so?

Write a Diary Entry

The day after Allie's father gave her a basketball was a big day for Allie. Write a diary entry that Allie might have written about her day. Tell about the events from Allie's point of view. Use a chart like this one to organize your ideas.

Writing CONNECTION

IMPORTANT EVENT	DETAILS	HOW ALLIE FEELS
1.		
2.		
3.		

Make Up a Routine

Music/Physical
Education
CONNECTION

Athletes in all sports spend hours practicing. Often they practice to music. Choose a recorded song and make up an exercise routine that you and a group of friends can do to the beat of the music. Demonstrate the routine to the class.

Music/Physical
Education
CONNECTION

Create and Solve Word Problems

Math
CONNECTION

In the game of basketball, points are scored in different ways that are worth different numbers of points. Look at this chart to see how points are scored.

Create word problems about basketball. Tell how many baskets of each kind a player made. Ask how many points the player scored in all. Have a classmate solve your problems.

Type of Basket Scored	Number of Points
free throw	1 point
regular basket	2 points
three-point shot	3 points

127

Narrative Elements

Focus Skill

You know that **characters** are the people and animals you meet in a story. The main character in "Allie's Basketball Dream" is Allie. Other characters include her father, Keisha, Buddy, Sheba, Julio, and Domino.

How do you know what the characters in a story are like? The author can tell you directly but often does not. You may have to figure out what the characters are like from what they say and do. Reread page 104 of the selection. Then look at the chart.

Character: Allie's father				
What he does	+	**What he says**	=	**What he is like**
gives her a special gift kisses her on the nose		"Because I love you."		kind loving caring

Visit *The Learning Site!*
www.harcourtschool.com

See *Skills* and *Activities*

Test Prep
Narrative Elements

▶ **Read the story.**

Try Again

Jerry couldn't wait to try his new inline skates. Before long, though, he found out that it wasn't as easy as it looked. He wobbled and wiggled and banged into things.

Mike and some other boys laughed. "Look at Mr. Wobbles," called Mike.

"Stop that, Mike!" called out Kate. "You're a good skater *now*," she told Mike, "but you had to learn, just like Jerry." She spent the rest of the afternoon skating with Jerry. She gave him suggestions to help him skate better.

Now answer numbers 1 and 2. Base your answers on the story "Try Again."

1. Think about what Mike says and does in the story. Which word best describes Mike's character?

    A nice

    B mean

    C quiet

    D scared

Tip

Reread parts of the story that tell what this character says and does. What kind of person acts this way?

2. What is Kate like? What does she say and do that shows readers what she is like?

Tip

Give examples from the story of some things the character says and does that show what she is like.

▲ **The Olympic Games**

ancient

host

compete

stadium

record

ceremonies

medals

earned

Vocabulary Power

The next selection you will read is about the Olympic Games. Did you know that the idea for our modern Olympic Games came from the Olympic Games held in Greece long ago?

OLYMPIC GAMES Long ago, in **ancient** times, special games were held every four years in Greece. The **host**, the place that put on the games, was called Olympia. Athletes came from all over Greece to **compete**, or take part in the contests.

Today some sporting events take place in a **stadium**, a building with rows of seats built around an open field. The word *stadium* comes from the race track used in the original games.

▲
The ruins of the stadium where the ancient Olympic Games in Greece were held.

There were foot races, wrestling, boxing matches, horse races, and long jumps.

When an athlete finished an event in the best time ever, he set a **record** for that sport. Winners were shown to an audience during **ceremonies**, where a crown of leaves was placed on each winner's head.

Today, a winning athlete may win **medals**, shining pieces of metal with images or writing on them.

Many of the best athletes have been good enough to make money in their sport. They have worked hard and **earned** a living being the best in the world in their sport.

Vocabulary-Writing CONNECTION

How do you feel about sports and games? Do you like to **compete**? Why or why not? Write a paragraph to explain your point of view.

THE
OLYMPIC GAMES:
Where Heroes Are Made
by Nicolas Camacho

Expository Nonfiction

Expository nonfiction explains information and ideas.

In this selection, look for

- **sections with headings and subheadings.**

- **photos with captions.**

- **events that are real.**

THE OLYMPIC GAMES: Where Heroes Are Made

by Nicolas Camacho

The first Olympic Games took place in ancient Greece. They were held about every four years for more than one thousand years. The first written report of the Games was made in 776 B.C., and the Games were stopped in the year A.D. 393. The early games were made up of many of the sports that are in today's summer Olympic Games. In 1896 Baron de Coubertin of France brought the Games back to life. He believed that taking part in sports would make people healthier and stronger. He also felt that coming together for the Games would help the countries of the world learn to live in peace.

Chariot races at an ancient stadium

1928 Betty Robinson, the first woman to win an olympic gold medal in running.

At first, the Olympic Games included only summer sports. In 1924, the Olympic Committee started the Olympic Winter Games, which include skiing, bobsledding, ice skating, ice hockey, and other winter sports.

In the 1896 Games only men were allowed to compete. By 1908 women were officially a part of the Olympics. Little by little the number of women athletes has increased. Today almost half of the athletes are women. In most cases men and women compete in separate events.

Just as in ancient times, the Games are held every four years. The early Olympics were always held in Olympia, Greece. Now the Games are held in a different city each time. Over the years the cities of Helsinki, Rome, Mexico City, Montreal, Los Angeles, Seoul, Barcelona, Sydney, and many others have played host to the Games.

Each Olympics begins the same way, with the Olympic flag being carried into the stadium. The white flag has five rings—blue, black, red, yellow, and green. At least one of these colors is on the flag of every country in the world.

During the opening ceremonies many nations gather in the Olympic stadium to celebrate.

Athletes from the United States join in the parade of nations.

The parade of nations comes next. The countries march into the stadium in alphabetical order except for the host country, which comes last. The athletes of each country follow their flag. At the first modern Olympics, 311 athletes came from 13 countries. They competed in fewer than 30 events. At the 2000 Olympics, more than 10,000 athletes from 199 countries came to the Games. They competed in 28 sports and 300 events.

At right: *Australian Cathy Freeman lights the torch at the 2000 Olympic Games in Sydney.*

After all the athletes have entered the stadium, they wait for the Olympic torch to arrive. This tradition began with the early Games. Four months before the start of the Games, a torch is lit at the ancient site of Olympia. It is carried by air, by sea, and on land, being handed from one person to another along the way, until it reaches the new site of the Olympics. When the torch arrives, it is used to light a giant Olympic flame. The flame burns night and day until the Games are over.

Before the events can start, the athletes take an oath, or solemn promise. One athlete is chosen to hold a corner of the Olympic flag and say the Olympic oath for all the athletes. In the oath, the athletes promise to obey the rules for fair play.

Let the Games begin!

Track and Field

Who will finish first? In track events, the first person across the finish line gets the gold.

In ancient times track-and-field events made up most of the Olympic Games. In fact, the first time games were held in Olympia, the only events were sprints, or short, fast races.

Track events are races between runners. The first three runners to cross the finish line win the gold, silver, and bronze medals. Sprinters do not have to run very far, so they can use all their energy right from the start. In the longer races, the runners do not run as fast as sprinters because they have to keep running for a longer time.

Sprinting for Gold
EVELYN ASHFORD

Evelyn Ashford had a long, successful career in track events. Her success began in high school, when she was invited to join the all-boys track team. She could run faster than most of her teammates.

When it was time for college, Evelyn applied to the University of California at Los Angeles. She was one of the first women to get an athletic scholarship. The summer after her first year in college, she ran in her first of five Olympic Games.

In the 1984 Los Angeles Olympics, Ashford won her first gold medal in the 100-meter race. Her second came as a member of the 100-meter relay team. At the 1988 Seoul Games, her relay team won again. Ashford captured her final Olympic gold in 1992 in Barcelona. At age 35, she became the oldest American woman to win an Olympic gold medal in a track event.

Evelyn Ashford of the United States won the 100-meter sprint in 1984.

The Best 400-Meter Runner Ever

MICHAEL JOHNSON

When people talk about track stars, Jesse Owens and Carl Lewis come to mind. Michael Johnson wanted people to talk about him, too. He wanted to make history on the track. At the 1996 Atlanta Olympic Games, he made it happen.

Michael Johnson has made running history twice. In the 1996 Atlanta Games, he became the first man to win gold medals in both the 200-meter and 400-meter races. At the 2000 Sydney Olympics, Johnson again made history. With his gold medal victory, he became the first person to win the 400-meter race in two Olympics in a row. What a great way to end a twelve-year track career!

Michael Johnson made history twice as an Olympic runner, at the 1996 and the 2000 Summer Olympics.

Swimming

Johnny Weissmuller, swimming champion at the 1924 Olympics in Paris.

In the first modern Games, a swimmer could use any stroke in a race. Today, there are four types of Olympic swimming events. In the breaststroke, backstroke, and butterfly events, swimmers must use only that one type of stroke. In the freestyle event, swimmers can use any stroke they like. Swimmers almost always use the crawl in a freestyle race because it is the fastest stroke. As a result, this stroke is often called the *freestyle*.

The Olympics have made the names of many swimmers well known. Before Johnny Weissmuller played the role of Tarzan in the movies, he was known for the three swimming medals he won at the 1924 Games in Paris. Weissmuller helped make swimming popular as an Olympic sport.

Swimming Toward History

MARK SPITZ

Mark Spitz began swimming on a team at a very early age. By the time he was 10, he held his first world record. Later Mark began to train at California's Santa Clara Swim Club, which is known for its outstanding swim program. The butterfly became his best event.

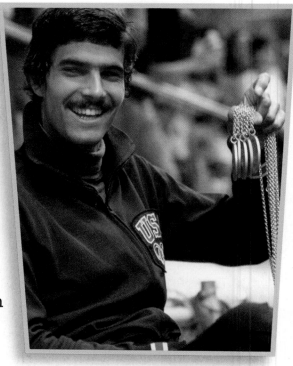

As a teenager he set world records in the freestyle and the butterfly. By 1968 Mark had set ten world records. After winning two gold medals at the Mexico City Games, Mark enrolled in college, where he trained even harder. He became captain of the swim team. By 1972 he was ready again for the Olympics.

Mark Spitz holds five of the seven gold medals he would win at the Munich Games, 1972.

At the Munich Games, Mark Spitz made Olympic history. He won seven gold medals—the most ever won in any sport in one Olympic Games. His first two gold medals were in the 100-meter and 200-meter freestyle. The next two were in the 100-meter and 200-meter butterfly events. He won the remaining three golds in relays. New world records were set in all seven races.

A Born Backstroker
LENNY KRAYZELBURG

At the 2000 Olympics, Lenny Krayzelburg took the lead on the first length of the 100-meter backstroke race. He never gave it up. In 52.73 seconds he set a new Olympic record. The gold medal was his!

Coaches had always told Lenny Krayzelburg he was a born backstroker. As a child in Odessa, Ukraine, Lenny had been chosen for a special training program. When he was eight, he was swimming five hours a day, running, and lifting weights. When he was thirteen, Lenny's parents decided to move to the United States.

The move to a new country was not easy for Lenny. He had to find a place to swim, and it was hard for him to get the training he needed. He knew he had found the right place when his new coach told him, "You can be the best in the world."

At the 2000 Sydney Games, he won all of his backstroke events—the 100-meter, the 200-meter, and the backstroke part of a relay race. The United States swim team won thirty-three medals in Sydney. Lenny Krayzelburg had earned three of the gold!

Lenny Krayzelburg shows off one of his three gold medals.

Team Sports

Just as in the ancient Olympics, new sports are always being added to the list of events. Unlike the early events, many of the new ones are team sports. Over the years, water polo, soccer, volleyball, basketball, field hockey, baseball, and softball have all joined the contests.

Volleyball was added to the list of Olympic events in 1964.

A Perfect Pitcher

LISA FERNANDEZ

In the summer of 2000, the United States softball team played fifty-seven games. The star pitcher, Lisa Fernandez, pitched five perfect games in a row. She struck out 162 hitters in 67 innings. Her record was 10–0.

Many people think Lisa Fernandez is the best softball pitcher in the world. Her windmill fastball travels at about 60 miles per hour. She is the pitcher no one wants to face. When Fernandez pitches, batters get very few hits. In the 1996 Olympic Games in Atlanta, one hit spoiled her team's perfect record, and she has never forgotten it. She didn't want that to happen in Sydney.

The game for the gold medal in Sydney was between the United States and Japan. Fernandez was pitching. By the fifth inning the score was 1–0 with Japan in the lead. In the second half of the inning, the United States was able to tie the game.

By the eighth inning Lisa Fernandez was doing what she does best—striking out batters. When the United States came up to bat, the game began to turn. Juri Takayama, a Japanese pitcher, walked the first two batters. Then Laura Berg popped a fly ball to the outfield. The ball fell into and then out of the outfielder's glove. The United States had won the gold!

Lisa Fernandez (right) displays her gold medal.

The Olympic Games end with special closing
ceremonies. Again the athletes gather on the field of
the Olympic stadium. The Olympic flag is handed from
the mayor of the host city to the mayor of the next
host city. It will be kept in the new city's town hall
until the next Games.

The president of the International Olympic
Committee called the Sydney 2000 Games "the best
Olympic Games ever." Then the Olympic flame was
put out, to be lit again in four years. The Olympic
Creed says, "The most important thing in the
Olympic Games is not to win but to take part. . . ."
Every Olympian agrees.

1 What kinds of events make up the Olympic Games, and what athletes **compete** in them?

2 How do the headings and subheads help you in reading this selection?

3 How might the Olympic Games change in the future?

4 If you could meet one of the athletes mentioned in the article, which one would you choose, and why?

5 What reading strategy helped you in reading this article? Tell how you used the strategy.

The Swi

by Constance Levy
illustrated by Kurt Nagahori

The sun
underwater
makes chains of gold
that rearrange
as I reach through.
I feel at home
within this world
of sunlit water, cool and blue.
I sip the air;
I stroke;
I kick;
big bubbles bloom as I breathe out.
Although I have no tail or fin
I'm closer than I've ever been
to what fish feel
and think about.

Making Connections

Compare Texts

1. What does the selection "The Olympic Games: Where Heroes Are Made" show about using talents and abilities?

2. Why does the author use some headings that name sports and other headings that name people?

3. How is the swimmer in the poem "The Swimmer" like Olympic gold-medal-winner Lenny Krayzelburg?

4. "The Swimmer" is a poem that does not rhyme. What is another poem you know that does not rhyme? Are the two poems alike in any other way?

5. What sources could you use to find out more about the events and athletes of the Olympic Games?

Write a Speech

After winning a medal, some athletes may make a short speech. Choose one of the athletes mentioned in "The Olympic Games." Write a speech three sentences long that the athlete might have given after winning his or her medal. Organize your ideas in this way for your sentences.

Writing CONNECTION

First sentence:	(how winning feels)
Second sentence:	(people to thank)
Third sentence:	(future goals)

Create a Fact Sheet

Social Studies CONNECTION

You learned in "The Olympic Games: Where Heroes Are Made" that athletes from 199 countries competed at the Sydney Olympics. Do research to find out about a country, other than the United States, that sends athletes to the Olympics. Create a fact sheet about the country's athletes, listing the most interesting facts you learn.

Draw an Athlete

Art CONNECTION

Many artists have created paintings or sculptures of athletes taking part in sports or games. Think about an athlete you read about in "The Olympic Games: Where Heroes Are Made." Draw or paint a picture of an athlete as he or she wins an Olympic event. You may want to show a runner crossing the finish line in a race or a diver diving from a diving board.

Elements of Nonfiction

"**T**he Olympic Games" is a nonfiction selection. It gives information about real people and real events.

Look at this chart to find out about different types of nonfiction writing.

Type of Nonfiction	What It Is Like
informational book or article	• gives information about a topic • is divided into sections with headings • may include photos with captions
biography	• is a true story of a person's life, written by another person • usually tells events in time order
autobiography	• is a true story of a person's life, written by that person • usually tells events in time order
newspaper story	• has a headline that gets attention • gives information about a recent event • tells *who? what? when? where? why? how?*
how-to article	• tells how to do something • tells what materials are needed • tells steps in the correct order

Visit *The Learning Site!*
www.harcourtschool.com

See *Skills* and *Activities*

Test Prep
Elements of Nonfiction

▶ **Read the paragraph. Then answer the questions.**

> If you are the first runner in a relay race, you will line up at the starting line. Listen for a signal that the race has begun. Then run as quickly as you can until you meet the next runner on your team.

1. Which statement is true about the paragraph?

   A It is written by a person to tell about his or her own life.

   B It is written by a person to tell about another person's life.

   C It tells how to do something.

   D It gives information about a recent event.

Tip

Read each choice. Look back at the paragraph each time to decide whether or not that choice is correct.

2. In which type of nonfiction selection would you expect to find the paragraph?

   F how-to article

   G autobiography

   H biography

   J newspaper story

Tip

Use your answer for number 1 to help you decide on the correct answer for number 2.

WHAT A TEAM!

CONTENTS

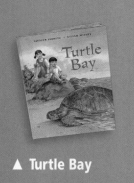

▲ Turtle Bay

Vocabulary Power

eager

trained

litter

patiently

message

wise

Many people love animals. At a pet show others can see what their pets can do.

Our Pet Show

Last Friday, our class had a pet show. The students were excited and **eager** to show off their pets.

Most of the pets were dogs and cats. Some people had **trained** their pets to do tricks. For example, Brianna taught her dog Bitsy to pick up **litter** from the ground and put it in the trash can! She told us it took a long time to teach Bitsy to do that. She said, "You have to work **patiently** to train a pet. This means waiting as long as it takes and not getting upset."

Some of the other pets in the show were a talking parakeet, a rabbit, and a goat named Gruff. Gruff's owner, Jake, said that he once got a call telling him that Gruff was eating a neighbor's flowers. As soon as he got that **message**, Jake ran out to bring Gruff home.

Our principal, Mrs. Dunn, visited our pet show. She said that taking care of pets can make us **wise**. It helps us understand important things such as how to be patient and unselfish.

Vocabulary–Writing CONNECTION

Some things cannot be done in a hurry. Write three sentences about something that has to be done **patiently**, and tell what would happen if you were impatient.

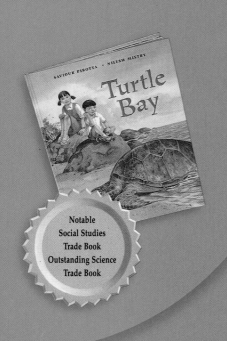

Genre

Realistic Fiction

Realistic fiction tells about characters and events that are like people and events in real life.

In this selection, look for

- characters who have a special friendship.

- events that occur in a real, but special setting.

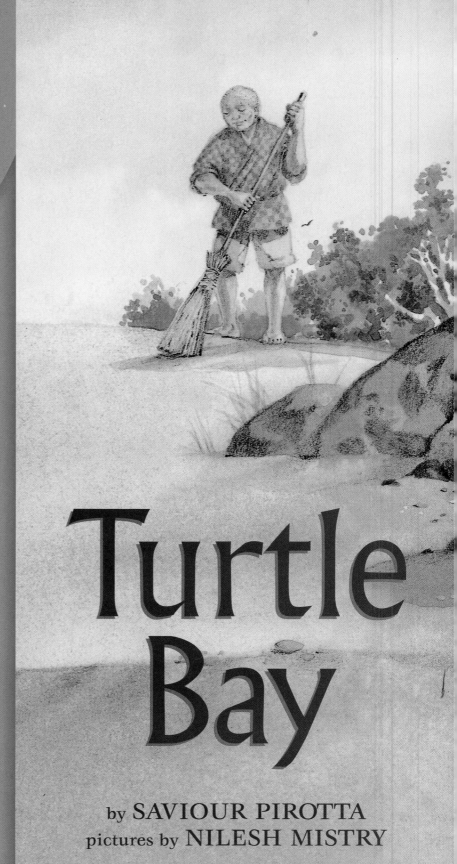

Turtle Bay

by SAVIOUR PIROTTA
pictures by NILESH MISTRY

Taro and Jiro-San were friends.

Jiro-San showed Taro how to feed crabs with pieces of rotten fish. He taught him to dive for sponges. When the sea was too rough for swimming, he trained him to sit very still and watch the sea horses swim around the seaweed in the deeper rock pools.

Taro's sister, Yuko, didn't like Jiro-San.

"He's weird," she said. "Last year my friends saw him sweeping the beach with a broom."

"No, he's not," said Taro. "He's old and wise, and full of wonderful secrets."

One day, Taro found Jiro-San sitting on a big rock. "What are you doing?" he asked.

"I am listening," said Jiro-San. "The wind is bringing me a message." Taro sat on the rock and listened. But all he could hear was the seagulls crying.

"Ah," said Jiro-San at last. "Now I understand . . . My old friends are coming."

"Who are your old friends?" asked Taro.

"You'll see," said Jiro-San.

Next day, Jiro-San brought two brooms and handed one to Taro.

"For sweeping the beach," he said.

Taro's heart sank. Yuko was right after all—Jiro-San was weird.

"There's a lot of rubbish and broken glass on the beach," Jiro-San explained. "My friends won't come if there is broken glass. They know they'll get hurt."

The boy and the old man swept the beach from one end to the other. They collected all the rubbish and put it in Jiro-San's cart. Soon the beach was cleaner than it had been all summer.

Jiro-San looked pleased.

"Meet me by the big rock tonight," he told Taro.

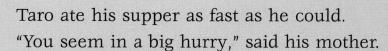

Taro ate his supper as fast as he could.

"You seem in a big hurry," said his mother.

"I am," said Taro. "Jiro-San's old friends are coming."

"Who are they?" his mother wanted to know.

"It's a secret," said Taro.

"What kind of secret?" Yuko asked.

Taro didn't answer. He washed his hands and went out to find Jiro-San.

"Look," said the old man, pointing out to sea. Taro saw a school of dolphins riding the waves.

"Are they your old friends?" he asked.

"No," said Jiro-San. "Perhaps they will come tomorrow night."

Taro waited patiently all the next day. In the evening, he met Jiro-San again. This time, the old man had brought his boat out of the shed. Jiro-San picked up the oars, and they pushed out to sea.

After a while, the old man said, "We've got company." Taro watched as a huge whale flicked her tail up out of the water. She had a calf swimming beside her.

"Are they your old friends?" Taro asked.

"They're friends," said Jiro-San, "but not the old friends I meant. Maybe they will come tomorrow."

The next evening, Jiro-San was in his boat again.

"Where are we going?" Taro wanted to know.

"Over there," said Jiro-San. He rowed out to a secret cove on a little island. There Taro saw three large fish with swords for snouts.

"Are they your old friends?" Taro asked.

"All fish are my friends," said Jiro-San. "But these aren't my old friends. They seem to be late this year. Perhaps they are not coming at all."

"Don't be sad," Taro said. "Perhaps they'll get here tomorrow."

"Do you want to come and wait for Jiro-San's old friends?" Taro asked Yuko after supper the next day. Yuko wasn't doing anything, so she followed Taro to the big rocks, kicking the sand as she walked.

"Ssshh," said Jiro-San. "I think they're here at last." Yuko and Taro saw a dark shape moving toward the shore. It was huge and bobbed up and down on the water like an enormous cork.

At last, the children could see what it was—a turtle!

"She's coming to lay her eggs on our beach," said Jiro-San proudly.

The turtle scrambled ashore and started digging with her flippers. When the hole was deep enough, she laid almost a hundred round, creamy-colored eggs in the nest. Then she filled in the hole with her hind flippers, flung more sand over it with her front flippers, and hurried back to the sea.

"She is going to tell the others," said Jiro-San.

"What is she going to tell them?" asked Yuko.

"That the beach is safe," said Taro happily.

The next day, Yuko came to the beach with her own broom.

"Can I help sweep the sand?" she asked.

"Of course," said Jiro-San. "The more of us there are, the safer the beach will be for the turtles."

The three friends swept up all the litter dropped by the beachgoers during the day. Then they sat on the rocks and watched more turtles coming ashore. There were lots of them, all huge and old and wise—just like Jiro-San.

"Now," said Jiro-San, "you must be patient, and wait until you hear from me again."

Eight weeks later, Jiro-San told the children to meet him at dusk.

"Sit on the rocks, please," he said, "and watch the ground."

The children looked and waited for what seemed like hours. As the moon rose, they saw something moving under the sand—something small and fast and eager.

"It's a baby turtle!" cried Taro. "The eggs have hatched!"

Soon the beach was full of baby turtles. There were hundreds of them, all scuttling down to the sea.

The children couldn't believe their eyes.

"Jiro-San is not crazy after all, is he?" Taro whispered to Yuko.

"No," said Yuko. "He is old and wise . . . and full of wonderful secrets."

THINK AND RESPOND

1. How do Jiro-San, Taro, and Yuko help the turtles?

2. What kind of person is Jiro-San? How can you tell?

3. What is the author showing you when Yuko brings her broom to the beach?

4. Would you have helped Jiro-San clean the **litter** from the beach? Tell why or why not.

5. How did using reading strategies help you understand events in the story?

Meet the Author
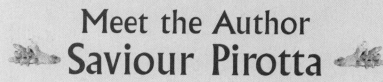
Saviour Pirotta

Saviour Pirotta's life as a writer began when he started writing plays for children. He read these plays on the radio in Malta, the island country in the Mediterranean Sea where he was born. Later, he moved to London, England.

Before he became a children's author, Saviour Pirotta worked as a storyteller. He told stories at many schools and libraries around England and became very well known. He has even told a story to Queen Elizabeth.

Now Saviour Pirotta has written many children's books. He says he likes to write books that teach children about things. When he has time, he visits schools to help children make their own picture books.

Visit *The Learning Site!*
www.harcourtschool.com

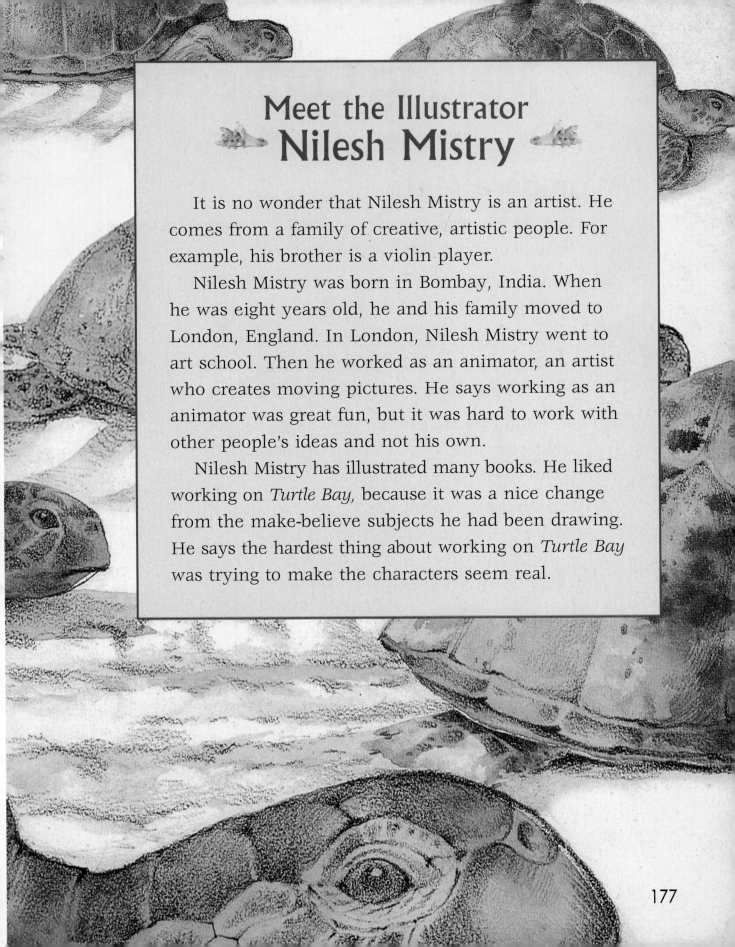

Meet the Illustrator
Nilesh Mistry

It is no wonder that Nilesh Mistry is an artist. He comes from a family of creative, artistic people. For example, his brother is a violin player.

Nilesh Mistry was born in Bombay, India. When he was eight years old, he and his family moved to London, England. In London, Nilesh Mistry went to art school. Then he worked as an animator, an artist who creates moving pictures. He says working as an animator was great fun, but it was hard to work with other people's ideas and not his own.

Nilesh Mistry has illustrated many books. He liked working on *Turtle Bay,* because it was a nice change from the make-believe subjects he had been drawing. He says the hardest thing about working on *Turtle Bay* was trying to make the characters seem real.

Making Connections

Compare Texts

1. Why do you think the story "Turtle Bay" belongs in a theme about working together as a team?

2. How does Yuko change between the beginning of the story and the end of the story?

3. Think of a story you know about a turtle or another creature. How are the animals in that story different from the animals in "Turtle Bay"? How are they alike?

4. What other realistic fiction story have you read in which someone helps an animal or animals? Which story seems more like real life? Why?

5. What more would you like to know about sea turtles? Where could you find this information?

Write About a Plan

Jiro-San, Taro, and Yuko clean the beach for the turtles. Think of a place that you and your friends could clean up, such as a beach, a park, or your schoolyard. Write a paragraph that tells your plan for cleaning up that place. Make a chart like this one so you can organize your ideas.

Writing CONNECTION

Supplies	Jobs
• garbage bags	• pick up litter

Create a 3-D Display

Jiro-San teaches Taro many new things about life in the ocean. Use an encyclopedia, the Internet, or a science textbook to research the nesting habits of the turtle. List 10 facts you learn. Then create a three-dimensional display.

Science CONNECTION

Draw Maps and Pictures

Look through the illustrations for "Turtle Bay." How would you describe the area or region? Look at maps of *your* area. Use what you know and what you learn to draw a picture that shows any special feature of the region where you live. Write a caption for your picture.

Social Studies CONNECTION

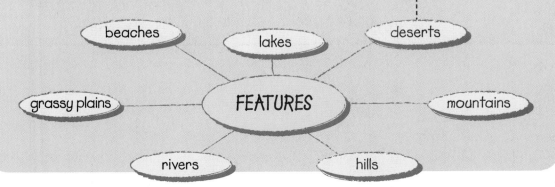

beaches · lakes · deserts · grassy plains · FEATURES · mountains · rivers · hills

Author's Purpose

Focus Skill

An author often has more than one purpose for writing. For example, Saviour Pirotta's main reason for writing "Turtle Bay" was to entertain readers. However, he might also have hoped to persuade readers to care for wildlife and the environment. Knowing the author's purposes can help you set your purpose for reading.

Look at this chart to learn more about an author's purposes for writing.

Author's Purpose	Examples of Writing for This Purpose	Reader's Purpose
to entertain	realistic fiction stories fantasy stories poetry	to enjoy to be entertained
to inform	nonfiction books biographies textbooks how-to books newsletters	to understand to be informed

to persuade	advertisements
	letters to a newspaper
	  editor
		to decide whether
		  or not to agree
		  with the author

Visit *The Learning Site!*
www.harcourtschool.com

See *Skills* and *Activities*

Test Prep
Author's Purpose

▶ **Read each paragraph and answer the question.**

Paragraph 1

Brushy brooms are the best you can buy! Whether you're sweeping indoors or outdoors, you'll do a better job with a Brushy broom!

1. **What is the author's purpose for writing Paragraph 1?**

    A to entertain

    B to inform

    C to persuade

    D to explain

Tip

Think about where you might see each kind of writing: in a picture book, a textbook, or an advertisement.

Paragraph 2

Sea turtles are found in warm waters around the world. They are different from land turtles in several ways. Sea turtles' legs are more like flippers. Another difference is that they cannot pull their heads and flippers into their shells.

2. **What is the author's purpose for writing Paragraph 2?**

    F to entertain

    G to inform

    H to persuade

    J to give directions

Tip

Try to answer the question without looking at the answer choices. Then see if your answer is given as one of the choices.

telegraph

drifts

trail

temperature

guided

splinters

Vocabulary Power

The next story tells about an event that happened in Alaska many years ago. These photos and captions will help you understand some important vocabulary.

The **telegraph** is a machine that was used to send coded messages from one place to another.

Alaska is a snowy place. Wind can blow the snow into large **drifts**, or piles. Some of these drifts can be very high.

The man stays on the **trail** so that he won't get lost. He must follow the path.

The **temperature** of something measures how hot or cold it is. In Alaska, on cold days, the average temperature in January could be 13°F.

This team of dogs has **guided** their owner across the land. The lead dog uses its sense of smell to lead the way.

People chop wood in Alaska to build fires to keep warm. Sharp, thin pieces of wood that come from logs and boards are called **splinters**.

Vocabulary–Writing CONNECTION

Write two sentences using the word **drifts**. In one sentence, use *drifts* as a noun. In the other sentence, use *drifts* as a verb. Use a dictionary if you need help.

Seven True Dog Stories
by MARGARET DAVIDSON
Pictures by SUSANNE SUBA

Award-Winning
Author

Genre

Narrative Nonfiction

Narrative nonfiction is a story that tells about real people or real events.

In this selection, look for

- an interesting historical event.

- events that are in time order.

184

BALTO, THE DOG WHO SAVED NOME

by Margaret Davidson   •   illustrations by Doug Rugh

"THIS IS NOME, ALASKA. REPEAT. THIS IS NOME, ALASKA. WE NEED HELP. FAST . . ."

A man bent over the machine in the Nome telegraph office. Again and again he pressed down the signal key. *Click-click-clack . . . Clack-click-clack . . .* He was sending a message to the town of Anchorage, Alaska, 800 miles to the southeast.

Click-click-clack . . . Clack-click-clack . . . The Anchorage telegraph operator wrote down the message. The news was very bad.

A terrible sickness had broken out in the Nome area—a disease called diphtheria. Some people had already died of it. Many more would die if they weren't treated soon.

There was no medicine to treat diphtheria in Nome. The medicine they needed would have to come from Anchorage—800 miles away— through a wild wind and snow storm. The storm was so bad that airplanes couldn't fly through it. Trains couldn't get through either. Nome was very near the sea, but the sea was frozen solid. And the road from the south was completely blocked by deep drifts of snow.

There was only one way to get the medicine from Anchorage to Nome—by dogsled.

ALASKA

Nome
Safety
Bluff
Golovin
Shaktoolik
Koyukuk
Ruby
Tolovana
Nenana
Kaltag
Anchorage

N
W E
S

0   100   200
Miles

The medicine was packed in a box and sent north by train—as far as a train could go on the snowy tracks. It was still more than 600 miles east of Nome. From now on teams of dogs would have to take it the rest of the way.

The teams were ready. The first team pushed north
through the storm to a little town. There a second team was
waiting. It went on to another small town where a third team
was ready to take the medicine farther.

At first the teams managed to go many miles before they grew tired. But the storm was growing worse by the minute. Finally Charlie Olson's team staggered into the little village of Bluff—60 miles from Nome. They had only gone 20 miles, yet Olson and the dogs were almost frozen and completely worn out.

Gunnar Kasson and his team were waiting in Bluff. The wind screamed through the little town. The snow was piling up deeper and deeper on the ground. It was 30 degrees *below* zero Fahrenheit outside now. And the temperature was falling fast.

"It's no use trying to go out in *that*," Charlie Olson said. "I almost didn't make it. You and the dogs will freeze solid before you get half way."

But Kasson knew how important the medicine was. He knew that hundreds—maybe thousands—of people would die if they didn't get the medicine soon. Besides, he knew he didn't have to go all the way. Another team was waiting 40 miles away in the little village of Safety. That team would take the medicine the last 20 miles to Nome.

Quickly Gunnar Kasson hitched up his team of dogs. And at the head of the long line he put his lead dog, Balto.

Balto was a mixed-breed. He was half Eskimo dog—and half wolf. Many dogs who are part wolf never become tame. They never learn to trust people—or obey them either. Balto was different. He was a gentle dog who obeyed orders quickly. He also knew how to think for himself.

Usually Gunnar Kasson guided the dogs. He told them where to go. Now he couldn't even see his hand in front of his face. So everything was up to Balto. The big black dog would have to find the trail by smell. Then he'd have to stay on it no matter what happened.

Gunnar Kasson climbed onto the back of the sled. He cracked his whip in the air. *"Mush!"* he cried. *"Move out!"*

The first part of the trail to Nome led across the sea ice.
This ice wasn't anything like ice on a small pond or lake.
It seemed much more *alive*. And no wonder. The water *under*
the ice was moving up and down because of the storm. So
the ice was moving up and down too. Up and down, up and
down it went, like a roller coaster.

In some places the ice was smooth—as smooth and slippery as glass. Dogs are usually sure-footed. But they slipped and skidded across this ice. So did the sled.

And sometimes the ice came to sharp points—points that dug deep into the dogs' paws.

Worst of all were the places where the ice was bumpy—so bumpy that the sled turned over again and again. Each time it turned over, the other dogs began to bark and snap at each other. But Balto always stood quietly while Kasson set the sled upright again. Balto was calm, so the other dogs grew calmer too.

The team had been moving across the ice for hours. Suddenly there was a loud *cracking* sound—like a gun going off. Kasson knew that sound. It was the sound of ice breaking. Somewhere not far ahead the ice had split apart. If the team kept going straight they would run right into the freezing water—and drown.

Balto heard the ice crack too. He slowed for a moment. Then he turned left. He headed straight out to sea. He went for a long time. Then he turned right once more.

Balto was leading the team *around* the icy water. Finally he gave a sharp bark and turned north. He had found the trail to Nome again.

Soon the trail left the sea ice. From now on it was over land. Things should have been easier. They weren't. The snow was falling thick and fast. In some places the wind swept most of it off the trail. But in other places the snow drifts came up almost over the dogs' heads. And the wind was blowing harder and harder. It sent bits of icy snow straight into Kasson's eyes. "I might as well have been blind," he said. "I couldn't even *guess* where we were."

And the dogs were so tired! Again and again they tried to stop. They wanted to lie down and go to sleep in the snow. Balto was just as tired. But he would not stop. He kept on pulling—and the other dogs had to follow behind.

Now something else began to worry Gunnar Kasson. They had been traveling for about 14 hours. Surely they should have reached the town of Safety in 14 hours. Kasson went on for another hour. Then he knew. Somehow they had missed the town in the storm. They must have passed right by the new dog team!

Kasson knew they couldn't stop and wait for the storm to die down. He and the dogs would freeze if they did. They couldn't go back to Bluff either. They had come too far. There was only one thing to do now. Pray . . . and push on to Nome.

Later Gunnar Kasson said he couldn't remember those last miles very well. Each one was a nightmare of howling wind and swirling snow and bitter cold. But somehow—with Balto leading slowly and steadily—they made it! At 5:30 in the morning, February 2, 1925—after 20 hours on the trail—the team limped into Nome!

The whole town was waiting for the medicine! They gathered around Gunnar Kasson. They shook his hand and pounded him on the back. "How can we ever thank you?" one woman cried.

Gunnar Kasson shook his head. Then he sank to his knees beside Balto. He began to pull long splinters of ice from the dog's paws. "Balto, what a dog," he said. "I've been in Alaska for 20 years and this was the toughest trip I've ever made. But Balto, *he* brought us through."

Many newspaper and magazine stories were written about Balto. His picture was printed on postcards and in books. And today, on a grassy hill in New York City's Central Park, there is a life-sized statue of Balto—the dog who saved Nome.

Think and Respond

1. How did Gunnar Kasson and Balto save the city of Nome?

2. How do the map and illustrations help you understand what it was like on the **trail** from Bluff to Nome?

3. How did Balto show that he was a good leader?

4. Who do you think was more of a hero, Gunnar Kasson or Balto?

5. Which reading strategies did you use with this story?

Meet the Author
Margaret Davidson

Dear Readers,

   I have been asked many times about how I came to be a writer. The first answer is that when I was a child I loved to read. You should like to read if you want to be a writer. Another reason is that my father was a writer, so I learned about writing early in my life.

   I have written many books and stories. I like writing about famous people such as Thomas Edison, George Washington, and Louis Braille. I like to write about animals, too. Some of my other books have been about dogs, dolphins, and horses.

   I hope you liked reading the exciting story of Balto's adventure in Alaska.

   Your friend,

   Margaret Davidson

   Margaret Davidson

 Visit *The Learning Site!*
www.harcourtschool.com

Sending

Before machines, an important message may have been sent like this:

By a runner

On horseback

By carrier pigeon

From one hilltop to another, by torches, flags, or hand signals

This time line shows some of the ways people have sent important messages. Today you can send a message almost anywhere in the world within minutes or even seconds. It was not always that easy!

1791 First machine is used to send a long-distance message. The arms are moved to show different letters of the alphabet.

1850s–1860s Telegraph lines are strung alongside railroad tracks. Telegraph offices open in every train station.

| 1790 | 1800 | 1810 | 1820 | 1830 | 1840 | 1850 | 1860 | 1870 |

1837 Samuel Morse invents a telegraph machine. Morse Code is used to tap out a message in dots and dashes.

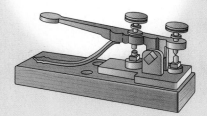

1866 Telegraph cables under the Atlantic Ocean link North America and Europe.

Atlantic Ocean

a **Message**

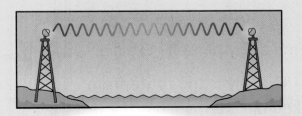

1980s Fax machines are used in many offices.

1927 First telephone call across the Atlantic Ocean uses radio waves instead of wires.

1956 Telephone cables are laid under the Atlantic Ocean.

1880 1890 1900 1910 1920 1930 1940 1950 1960 1970 1980 1990 **2000**

1876 Alexander Graham Bell invents the telephone.

1930s First phototelegraph sends copies of photographs and other pictures.

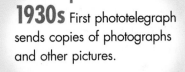

1990s Electronic mail (e-mail) allows people to send a message from one computer to another computer.

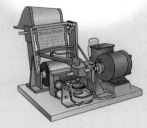

Think and Respond
What kind of information can you find on a time line?

Making Connections

Compare Texts

1 Could Balto have saved Nome all by himself? Explain.

2 Look at the map on page 187. Why is the route from Anchorage to Nenana marked differently from the rest?

3 Balto's journey took place in 1925. How does the time line on pages 200–201 help you understand why sending and receiving messages was so difficult?

4 Think of another true story you have read. Which selection was more exciting to read, and why?

5 What else would you like to find out about dogsledding? Write down three questions. Then tell where you would look to find each answer.

Write a Postcard

Gunnar Kasson and his dogs finally arrived in Nome after twenty hours on the trail. Write a message that Kasson might have written on a postcard to his family. Jot down your ideas in a graphic organizer like this one.

Dear _____,

Name
City, State
Zip Code

Writing CONNECTION

202

Make a Temperature Graph

Alaska's frigid winter weather made travel almost impossible. Use an almanac to find the average high temperature for January in Anchorage, Alaska. Find the city in the world that has the highest average temperature for January. Make a bar graph that compares the temperatures.

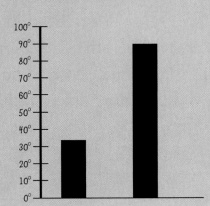

Social Studies/Math CONNECTION

Make an Informational Chart

Balto is trained to help people by pulling a dog sled. Use encyclopedia articles and nonfiction books to find out about other types of dogs that are used for work. Then make a chart to compare the types of dogs and the jobs they are trained to do. Why is each type of dog best for its job?

Science CONNECTION

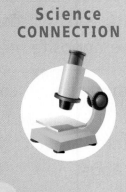

Word Relationships

Focus Skill

Authors use related words to tell about people, places, and events. You need to understand how words are related in order to understand what the author is telling you or describing to you. This chart shows some ways in which words are related to each other.

How Words Are Related	Examples
synonyms: words that have similar meanings	The first team pushed north to a <u>little</u> town. The second team went on to another <u>small</u> town.
antonyms: words that have opposite meanings	In some places the ice was <u>smooth</u>. In other places the ice was <u>bumpy</u>.
homophones: words that sound the same but have different meanings and spellings	Nome was near the <u>sea</u>. Blowing snow made the trail hard to <u>see</u>.

When you read, think about how words are related. Use the context to figure out word meanings.

Test Prep
Word Relationships

▶ **Read the passage. Then answer the questions.**

> The rain poured down. The horses and riders were <u>soaked</u>, but still they kept going. They had to reach the city before dark, even though their clothes and packs were wet. Carla rode at the head of the line. With the rain in her eyes, she could hardly see the road <u>before</u> her. She hoped her horse, Ruby, knew the way. The other riders behind her hoped so, too. Carla whispered into Ruby's ear, "You can do it, Ruby. I know you can!"

1. **Which word in the paragraph is a synonym for <u>soaked</u>?**

   A rain

   B poured

   C leaned

   D wet

Tip

Think about what the word means. Look for a word with the same or a similar meaning.

2. **Which word in the paragraph is an antonym for <u>before</u>?**

   F still

   G behind

   H down

   J hardly

Tip

Think about what the word means. Look for a word with the opposite meaning.

curious

creature

delicate

survived

marine

collapsed

Vocabulary Power

Did you ever see something strange and wonder what it was? Here is what happened when some animals found something strange.

HEN: What are you looking at?

PIG: We don't know, Hen.

DUCK: We are very **curious**. We're full of questions about this thing we found.

HEN: Let me take a look.

HEN: This is a strange **creature**. I've never seen an animal like this before.

HORSE: Do you think it fell from the sky?

GOAT: If it did, it must be very strong. If it were **delicate**, it would have broken.

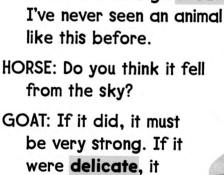

COW: It's still alive. It must be strong if it **survived** a fall from the sky!

HEN: Maybe it's a **marine** animal, all the way from the sea.

PIG: What would a sea creature be doing here?

HEN: It must have crawled here, looking for water. It got so weak that it just fell down. It **collapsed**. Go get the poor thing some water!

PORCUPINE: Silly farm animals! Haven't you seen a porcupine before? I didn't fall from the sky. I didn't come from the sea. I just wanted to take a little nap!

Vocabulary–Writing CONNECTION

Marine animals live in the seas and oceans. Write about one marine animal that you are **curious** about. What questions do you have about the animal?

WILD

They're

from *Ranger Rick Magazine*

by Tui De Roy

SHOTS,
My Life

"Hey, you don't scare me," this Galapagos penguin seems to be saying. But who *is* that strange, masked creature?

The creature behind the face mask (on page 209) is me. Most of the time, you'll find me behind a camera. Come see the world through my eyes.

When I was a little girl, all my best friends were furry, feathered, or scaly! My friends were the gentle, trusting creatures of the Galapagos (gə·lä´pə·gəs) Islands, where I grew up.

In those days there was no school nearby, so my mom taught my little brother and me at home. But my favorite classroom was the great Galapagos outdoors! The islands were formed long ago by a bunch of volcanoes far out in the Pacific Ocean. My family moved to the islands from Europe when I was only two.

When I was 10, my dad let me use his old camera. Right away, I started snapping photos of my animal friends. And in the 30 years since then, I've never stopped.

The best part was that the animals in the Galapagos were as curious about me as I was about them. That's why I was able to get "up close and personal" with the Galapagos hawks shown here. See the shot I got? **(above)**

Like I said, I'm still taking lots of wildlife photos, and my best friends are still furry, feathered, and scaly. But now I find them all over the world, not just in the Galapagos.

I like to photograph animals best when they're minding their own business—not watching me. That means I have to spend a lot of time with them until they get so used to me that they forget I'm there.

Now let me tell you about some of my favorite photos— and the adventures I had getting them.

ENOUGH, ALREADY!

The king penguin chick **below** looks like it's wearing a furry overcoat. But that's just its thick, downy baby feathers. They work like a coat to keep the chick warm.

The chick was bugging its parents, begging for food. They finally got tired of being pestered and started waddling away. But the chick kept right up with them, and I had to scurry to get this shot.

HEY, OUTTA MY WAY!

The Galapagos Islands are famous for their huge tortoises. In fact, *galapagos* means "tortoises" in Spanish. When early Spanish-speaking explorers came to the islands, they saw *tons* of these big fellas.

One day I was nose to nose with one, with just a camera between us **(top)**. The tortoise was so busy looking for just the right tasty plants, it acted as if I weren't even there. I had to move out of *its* way before it bumped right into me! But look at the kind of action shot you can snap by getting down with your subject **(above)**. *CHOMP.* Tortoises love a good cactus. Never mind the spines!

INTO THE WASH

Galapagos marine iguanas (i·gwä′nəz) are the only lizards in the world that feed in the sea. Usually they graze on stubby seaweed that grows along the wave-beaten shoreline.

I wanted to show how these little sea dragons are right at home in the pounding waves. But to do it, I had to get in there with them! First I put my camera into a waterproof case with a clear front clamped on. Then I crept toward my target **(above)**. Iguanas have sharp claws, so they can hang on tight to rocks in the surf. What about me? I bounced around and got lots of cuts and bruises. But this neat photo **(right)** was worth it!

DUELING DUOS

Watching animals fight can be pretty wild—and scary. But usually it looks worse than it is: The fighters almost never hurt each other seriously.

Look at the two male frigate birds in the big photo **above**. They were squabbling Galapagos neighbors, snapping at each other with their sharp beaks. But neither delicate throat pouch got punctured. (The male on the right had his pouch puffed out, showing off to the females flying overhead.)

The fight in the **lower** photo was between elephant seal bulls on an island near Antarctica. I saw these guys having it out from way down the beach. They were so wrapped up in who would be beach-master, they didn't notice me getting close. (But not *too* close. Each bull was taller than me and outweighed me by a couple of tons!)

In a few months, her babies would hatch and, with luck, head out to sea too. The ones that survived would spend years growing up far out in the ocean. Then someday the females would return to this beach to lay their eggs.

Like the sea turtles, I return to the shores of the Galapagos Islands from time to time too. There are always new animal friends to meet there.

All of a sudden, they reared up and flashed their "fangs." *CLICK*— got it! I had to be really quick. The next second, they were back to their lazy pushing and shoving. Finally, they collapsed into a heap and started snoozing.

HOMECOMING

The shot **above** was taken at sunrise on a Galapagos beach. The green turtle was crawling back down to the sea. She had spent the night burying her eggs in the sand.

Think and Respond

1 How is the author able to take close-up photographs of animals?

2 Some words in this article are in color. How do these words help the reader?

3 Why does the author say that wild shots are her life?

4 How would you feel about getting very close to a wild **creature**, as the author does?

5 What reading strategies did you find helpful as you read this article? Give examples.

A Place of Their Own

from *Contact Kids* magazine

by Carol Pugliano

Popcorn Park Zoo is a very special place for animals. John Bergmann is the zoo's general manager. He and his staff save wild animals who are hurt. They take the animals to Popcorn Park Zoo in Forked River, New Jersey, where they can live and get better.

Popcorn Park wasn't always a zoo. Twenty years ago, it was called the Forked River Animal Care Center. The Center found homes for cats and dogs.

Then along came Rigby the raccoon. One day, Bergmann got a call from a woman who had found a raccoon in her backyard. Its leg was caught in a trap. The animal had dragged itself from the woods to the woman's house.

Bergmann and a man from the New Jersey Humane Society rescued Rigby from the trap. But the raccoon's leg was *so badly hurt, its front* paw had to be removed.

Without his paw, Rigby couldn't find food or defend himself. So he couldn't be released into the wild. Instead, Bergmann built Rigby a tree house at the Animal Care Center—and the zoo was born!

Out of the Wild

Today, more than 250 animals call the Popcorn Park Zoo home. Almost all of them have a story to tell. There are deer that have been hit by cars and only have three legs. There are pot-bellied pigs that grew too big to be pets. There are bears, lions and other circus animals that have been treated badly.

Many zoo residents, like Cindy Lou the cougar, are wild animals that people found and kept. Thinking she could be raised like a pet, Cindy Lou's owners had her teeth filed down and her claws removed. But the owners soon realized that wild animals aren't meant to be pets. They wanted to get rid of Cindy Lou. But she couldn't be returned to the wild. Popcorn Park Zoo gave Cindy Lou a second chance at a happy life.

Other residents are wild animals that have been hurt. Bergmann and the zoo's staff take care of these animals. Most of them become well enough to be released back into the wild. That's Bergmann's favorite part about working at the zoo. "There's nothing better than seeing the white tail of a deer as it runs back into the woods," he told *Contact Kids*. "It's a really good feeling."

Think and Respond

How does Popcorn Park Zoo help animals?

Making Connections

Compare Texts

1 How does "Wild Shots, They're My Life" fit in this theme about working as a team?

2 How are the headings on pages 212 and 213 different from the headings on the other pages?

3 After reading "Wild Shots, They're My Life" and "A Place of Their Own," which one would you be more likely to tell someone about? What would you say?

4 Think about another job some adults have. How is that job similar to and different from Tui De Roy's job as a photographer?

5 What questions would you ask the author of this article if you could meet her?

Write a Paragraph

Writing CONNECTION

Tui De Roy takes photographs of animals. Brainstorm other jobs that have to do with animals. You might write your ideas in a web like the one shown here. Then choose the job you would most like to have. Write a paragraph telling which job you chose and why.

Zookeeper

Wildlife Photographer

Animal Careers

Animal Trainer

Draw a Diagram

Science CONNECTION

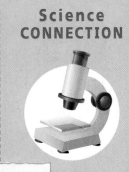

In "Wild Shots," Tui De Roy included a number of photographs of animals searching for food. Choose an animal from the selection. Look in a science textbook or use an encyclopedia in print or on CD-ROM to learn about the food chain for that animal. Make a diagram that shows the food chain and the animal's place in it.

Artistic Points of View

Art CONNECTION

Tui De Roy shoots photos of animals from many different angles. For example, on page 213, she is shooting a picture at ground level, "nose to nose" with a tortoise. Cut out two or three interesting photos from old magazines. For each photo, draw a picture to show the point of view from which you think the photographer took the picture.

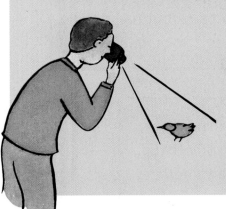

Author's Purpose

What is Tui De Roy's main purpose in "Wild Shots, They're My Life"? She gives information about her career and about the creatures she has photographed. Her main purpose is to inform readers about these topics.

How can you identify an author's purpose? Look at this web for some ideas.

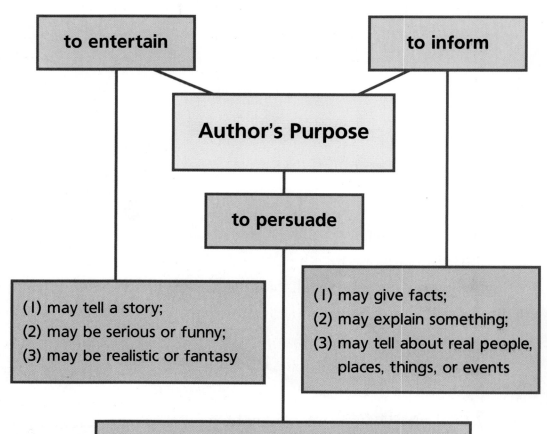

| to entertain | | to inform |

Author's Purpose

to persuade

(1) may tell a story;
(2) may be serious or funny;
(3) may be realistic or fantasy

(1) may give facts;
(2) may explain something;
(3) may tell about real people, places, things, or events

(1) may try to get you to buy something;
(2) may tell you that you should do something;
(3) may want you to think or believe something

Test Prep
Author's Purpose

▶ **Read each paragraph.**

A   Most lizards are meat eaters, but iguanas eat only plants. Some iguanas live in trees, and some live in desert regions. The marine iguana of the Galápagos Islands is the only type of iguana that feeds in the sea.

B   Terri the Tortoise was tired. She had spent the whole day making cactus sandwiches for the big party tomorrow. "I'll just take a little nap," said Terri.

Now answer numbers 1 and 2.

1. **What is the author's main purpose in paragraph A? How can you tell?**

Tip

Decide whether the author is telling a story, giving facts, or suggesting that you should do something or think in a certain way.

2. **What is the author's main purpose in paragraph B? How can you tell?**

Tip

Ask yourself what type of writing this paragraph might be from and what the author's purpose usually is for that type of writing.

▲ **Little Grunt and the Big Egg**

omelet

brunch

peaceful

escape

erupting

lava

Vocabulary Power

In "Little Grunt and the Big Egg," a family plans a nice meal and gets a big surprise instead. Use these scenes to help you predict what will happen in the coming story.

The cook makes an **omelet**. He beats eggs and adds other ingredients. Then he cooks the omelet in a pan.

Some people like to have omelets for **brunch**, a combined late breakfast and early lunch.

This mountain looks calm and quiet. You might not even know that this **peaceful** mountain is a volcano.

Now it looks as if something is about to happen. If you were nearby, this would be a good time to **escape** and get away from the danger.

The volcano is **erupting**. It is blowing out hot gases and rocks. You can see streams of hot, melted rock called **lava** flowing down the mountain's side. Now aren't you glad you escaped in time?

Vocabulary-Writing CONNECTION

Write a short paragraph that describes a place that you think is **peaceful**. What does it look like? What sounds do you hear?

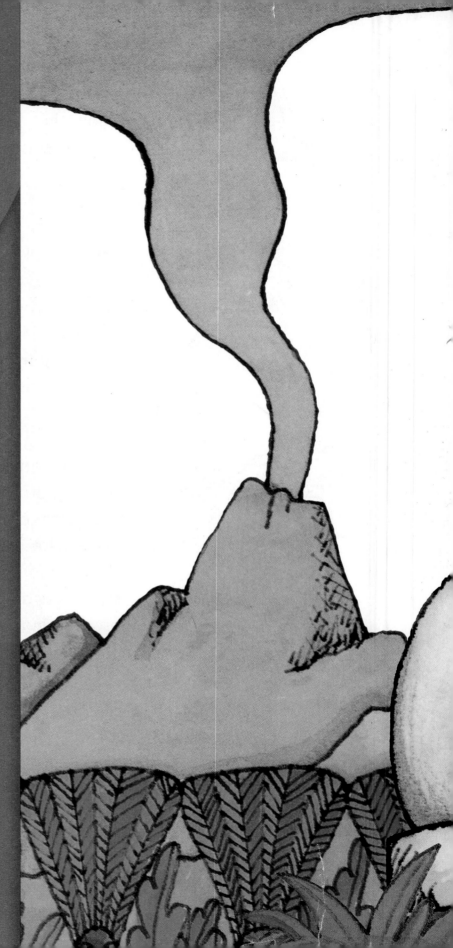

Award-Winning
Author and
Illustrator

Fantasy

A fantasy is a story
or daydream very
different from reality.

In this selection, look for

- events that could not
  really happen.

- characters that
  may or may not be
  realistic.

Little Grunt
and the
Big Egg

by Tomie
dePaola

Once upon a time, in a big cave, past the volcano on the left, lived the Grunt Tribe. There was Unca Grunt, Ant Grunt, Granny Grunt, Mama Grunt, and Papa Grunt. Their leader was Chief Rockhead Grunt. The smallest Grunt of all was Little Grunt.

One Saturday morning, Mama Grunt said to Little Grunt, "Little Grunt, tomorrow the Ugga-Wugga Tribe is coming for Sunday brunch. Could you please go outside and gather two dozen eggs?"

"Yes, Mama Grunt," said Little Grunt, and off he went.

At that time of year, eggs were hard to find. Little Grunt looked and looked. No luck. He was getting tired.

"What am I going to do?" he said to himself. "I can't find a single egg. I'll try one more place."

And it was a good thing that he did, because there, in the one more place, was the biggest egg Little Grunt had ever seen.

It was too big to carry. It was too far to roll. And besides, Little Grunt had to be very careful. Eggs break *very* easily.

Little Grunt thought and thought.

"I know," he said. He gathered some of the thick pointy leaves that were growing nearby. He wove them into a mat. Then he carefully rolled the egg on top of it. He pulled and pulled and pulled the egg all the way home.

"My goodness," said the Grunt Tribe. "Ooga, ooga, what an egg! That will feed us *and* the Ugga-Wuggas. And even the Grizzler Tribe. Maybe we should invite *them* to Sunday brunch, too."

"I'll be able to make that special omelet I've been wanting to," said Mama Grunt.

"Ooga, ooga! Yummy! Yummy!" said all the Grunts.

They put the egg near the hearth, and then they all went to bed.

That night, by the flickering firelight, the egg began to make noise. CLICK, CRACK went the egg. CLICK, CRACK, CLUNK. A big piece fell to the floor. CLICK, CRACK, CLUNK, PLOP. The egg broke in half, and instead of the big egg sitting by the fire . . .

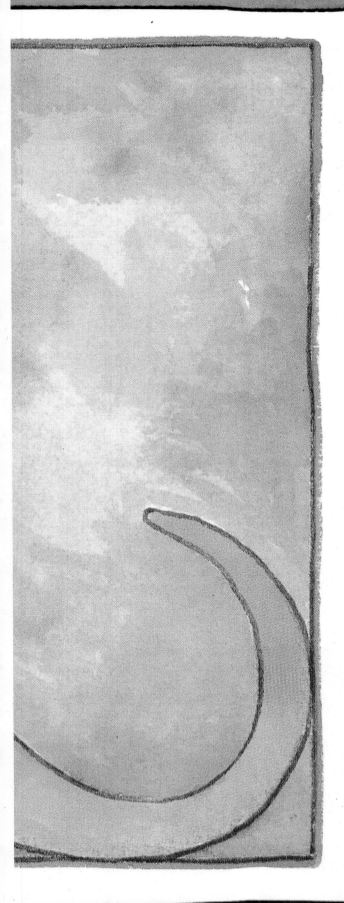

There was a baby dinosaur!

"Waaangh," cried the baby dinosaur. And all the Grunt Tribe woke up.

"Ooga, ooga!" they said. "What are we going to do?"

"There goes the brunch!" said Unca Grunt.

"What will the Ugga-Wuggas say?" said Ant Grunt.

"I bet I'm allergic to that thing," said Papa Grunt.

Chief Rockhead Grunt said, "All I know is it can't stay . . ."

But before he could finish, Little Grunt said, "May I keep him? Please? *Please?*"

"Every boy needs a pet," said Granny Grunt.

Some of the Grunts said yes. Some of the Grunts said no. But it was finally decided that Little Grunt could keep the baby dinosaur.

"Against my better judgment," mumbled Chief Rockhead Grunt.

"Oh, well, I suppose I can make pancakes for Sunday brunch," said Mama Grunt.

"I'm going to call him George," said Little Grunt.

Little Grunt and George became great pals.

But there was a problem. The cave stayed the same size, but George didn't. He began to grow.

And GROW.
And **GROW.**

The cave got very crowded.

And there were other problems. George wasn't housebroken. George ate ALL the leaves off ALL the trees and ALL the bushes ALL around the cave. But still he was hungry. George liked to play—rough. George stepped on things. And when he sneezed—well, it was a disaster.

"Ooga, ooga! Enough is enough!" said the Grunts.

"Either that dinosaur goes, or I go," said Unca Grunt.

"I spend all day getting food for him," said Ant Grunt.

"Achoo!" said Papa Grunt. "I told you I was allergic to him."

"He stepped on all my cooking pots and broke them," said Mama Grunt.

"I guess it wasn't a good idea to keep him," said Granny Grunt. "How about a nice *little* cockroach. They make nice pets."

"I'm in charge here," said Chief Rockhead Grunt. "And I say, *That giant lizard goes!*"

"Ooga, ooga! Yes! Yes!" said all the Grunts.

"But you promised," said Little Grunt.

The next morning, Little Grunt took George away from the cave, out to where he had found him in the first place.

"Good-bye, George," said Little Grunt. "I'll sure miss you."

"Waaargh," said George.

Big tears rolled down both their cheeks. Sadly, Little Grunt watched as George walked slowly into the swamp.

"I'll never see him again," sobbed Little Grunt.

The days and months went by, and Little Grunt still missed George. He dreamed about him at night and drew pictures of him by day.

"Little Grunt certainly misses that dinosaur," said Mama Grunt.

"He'll get over it," said Papa Grunt.

"It's nice and peaceful here again," said Ant and Unca Grunt.

"I still say a cockroach makes a nice pet," said Granny Grunt.

"Ooga, ooga. Torches out. Everyone in bed," said Chief Rockhead.

That night, the cave started to shake. The floor began to pitch, and loud rumblings filled the air.

"Earthquake!" cried the Grunts, and they rushed to the opening of the cave.

"No, it's not," said Granny Grunt. "Look! Volcano!"

And sure enough, the big volcano was erupting all over the place. Steam and rocks and black smoke shot out of the top. Around the cave, big rocks and boulders tumbled and bounced.

"We're trapped! We're trapped!" shouted the Grunts. "What are we going to do?"

"Don't ask me!" said Chief Rockhead. "I resign."

"Now we have no leader," cried Ant Grunt.

"Now we're really in trouble!" shouted Papa Grunt.

The lava was pouring out of the volcano in a wide, flaming river and was heading straight for the cave.

There wasn't enough time for the Grunts to escape. All of a sudden, the Grunts heard a different noise.

"Waaargh! Wonk!"

"It's George," cried Little Grunt. "He's come to save us."

"Ooga, ooga! Quick!" said the Grunts as they all jumped on George's long neck and long back and long tail.

And before you could say Tyrannosaurus rex, George carried them far away to safety.

"As your new leader," Papa Grunt said, "I say this is our new cave!"

"I like the kitchen," said Mama Grunt.

"Now, when I was the leader . . ." said Plain Rockhead Grunt.

"When do we eat?" said Unca Grunt.

"I can't wait to start decorating," said Ant Grunt.

"I always say a change of scenery keeps you from getting old," said Granny Grunt.

"And George can live right next door," said Little Grunt.

"Where is George?" asked Mama Grunt. "I haven't seen him all afternoon."

"Ooga, ooga. Here, George," called the Grunts.

"Waaargh," answered George.

"Look!" said Little Grunt.

"Oh no!" said the Grunts.

There was George, sitting on a pile of big eggs.

"I guess I'd better call George Georgina!" said Little Grunt.

And they all lived happily ever after.

Think and Respond

1. How do Little Grunt's family members feel about George in the beginning?

2. How can you tell that this story couldn't really happen?

3. Why does Little Grunt say he'd better call George Georgina?

4. Do you think the Grunts' lives will be **peaceful** from now on? Why or why not?

5. What reading strategies did you use as you were reading this story? How did a strategy help you understand the story?

Meet the Author and Illustrator
Tomie dePaola

Tomie dePaola has always had a talent for art. Even as a small child, Tomie was good at drawing. "I guess I saw things differently than most of my school friends. . . . I saw with my eyes like everyone else but I also saw 'inside' with 'inner eyes.' My mother told me that was imagination."

Tomie dePaola's other great talent is for telling stories. When he was a boy, there was no television. He listened to stories his mother read aloud, and he learned about storytelling from her. There was also the radio. Every Saturday morning Tomie listened to his favorite show, "Let's Pretend," and let his imagination grow.

Tomie dePaola enjoyed taking art classes in high school and decided to go on to art school. Afterward, he knew he wanted to make children's books, and he showed his work to many publishers. It's hard to believe now that it was six years before he was asked to illustrate a book!

Visit *The Learning Site!*
www.harcourtschool.com

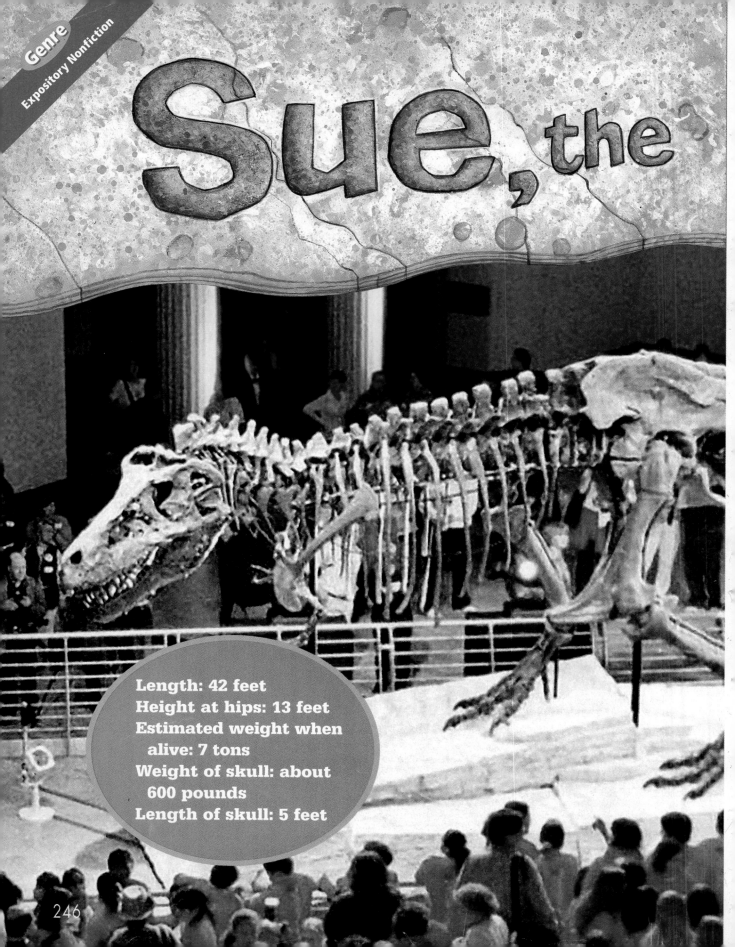

Sue, the

Length: 42 feet
Height at hips: 13 feet
Estimated weight when
  alive: 7 tons
Weight of skull: about
  600 pounds
Length of skull: 5 feet

Tyrannosaurus Rex

by Andrew Keown

Sue Who?

In the spring of 2000, the Field Museum in Chicago, Illinois, opened one of its grandest shows ever. Visitors poured in to see the largest and most complete dinosaur fossil found so far.

Although no one knows whether the dinosaur was a male or a female, it is called Sue. Here's why.

Where Sue Was Found

On a hot summer day in 1990, a woman named Sue Hendrickson was working with a team of fossil hunters near Faith, South Dakota. While some of the team went into a nearby town, Hendrickson stayed behind to look for fossils. What she found that day would be one of the greatest fossil discoveries ever made.

Hendrickson wandered over to some cliffs she had noticed earlier. Fossils are usually hidden in the earth, but she came across some pieces of bone lying on the ground. They looked very old. Where did they come from? The fossil hunter looked upward to the cliffs above her. Perhaps the bones had fallen from there.

Hendrickson spotted some strange bones sticking partway out of the cliff-side. The bones were huge! At once, she believed that they belonged to one of the largest and perhaps strongest dinosaurs that had ever lived. The *Tyrannosaurus rex!*

Here's the spot where Sue Hendrickson found those first pieces of bone.

When the other fossil hunters returned to the site, Hendrickson showed them the bones. They agreed that this amazing find was indeed a *T. rex.* (*T. rex* is a shorter name for *Tyrannosaurus rex*.) They named it Sue, after the woman who found it.

This museum worker is working on clearing the rock away from Sue's lower jaw.

Sue Goes to the Museum

In 1997 the Field Museum, with the help of some investors, paid $8.36 million for Sue. This was a very important buy. The museum plans to always keep the Sue exhibit open to the public. This will allow people to visit it and learn about natural history, or the history of our natural world. Scientists will be allowed to study Sue as well, so that they can learn more about the past.

It took two years for a museum team to strip rock from the bones. Team members also made models to replace some of the missing bones, using what they know from other dinosaur skeletons. Almost 90% of Sue's skeleton was found, which makes it the most complete *T. rex* skeleton today. Since the first discovery in 1900, twenty-two *T. rex* skeletons have been found. Only seven of those are more than half complete.

249

This is the top half of Sue's skull after it had been partly cleaned.

What Sue Can Teach Us

How have scientists learned from Sue's discovery? First, they gathered facts by making measurements and looking closely at the bones. They put the facts together with what they already knew about animals, and they drew some conclusions.

Even with such a gigantic head, the *T. rex* had a very small brain. The brain cavity, or the area where the brain was, is just large enough to hold about one quart of milk. The olfactory bulbs, which control the sense of smell, are very large. This tells scientists that the *T. rex* may not have been very smart, but it was probably able to smell its prey from a great distance.

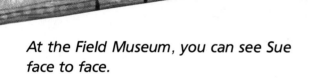

At the Field Museum, you can see Sue face to face.

The teeth of the *T. rex* are long and sharp. They measure from $7\frac{1}{2}$ to 12 inches long. The length and shape of its teeth tell scientists that the *T. rex* was probably a meat eater. A plant eater would not need such big, sharp teeth.

Scientists have also learned about the Earth from studying the area where they found Sue. They have found fossils of plants in that area. Because of these fossils, scientists believe that 67 million years ago South Dakota was warmer and wetter than it is today. It seems that the plant-eating dinosaurs in the area had plenty to eat before they became meals for *T. rex*.

Sue Today

The museum officials thought about ways to show Sue. They wanted visitors to leave with a feeling they would never forget. Look at the photographs of Sue. Imagine the dinosaur crouching over. Maybe it was eating. Maybe it was looking for something on the ground. With its head turned to the side, maybe it had just heard a noise. Did it also see something? How would you feel if it had just seen you? Chances are, you would never forget it!

THINK AND RESPOND
What makes Sue such an important find?

251

Making Connections

Compare Texts

1. How do Little Grunt and George work together in "Little Grunt and the Big Egg"?

2. Why does the cave seem smaller as George begins to grow?

3. How is the dinosaur that you read about in "Sue, the Tyrannosaurus Rex" different from George, the dinosaur in "Little Grunt and the Big Egg"?

4. Why did you like this story more or less than other fantasy stories you have read?

5. What is the most recent dinosaur discovery you have heard about or read about? Where would you look to find out about the latest dinosaur research?

Write an Advertisement

Imagine that Georgina's eggs have hatched and that the baby dinosaurs are ready to go to new homes. Write an advertisement that Little Grunt might post to find good homes for the little dinosaurs. Use a list like this one to organize your ideas for the advertisement.

Writing CONNECTION

BABY DINOS FOR SALE
- (how many)
- (description)
- (price)
- (name and phone number)

Create a Cave Dwelling

Little Grunt lived in a cave with his tribe. Early humans are often called "cave dwellers" because there is evidence that they lived in caves. Do some research on early cave dwellers. Find out what we know about their family life and what clues have been found to show how they lived. Then draw or create a scene that shows some of the facts you learned. On a card, write a caption for your scene. Attach the card to your scene.

Make a Chart

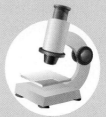

We know that "Little Grunt and the Big Egg" is fantasy because people could never have had dinosaurs for pets. Do research to find out how, long ago, different kinds of dinosaurs lived and when they became extinct. Use an encyclopedia or nonfiction books for your research. Make a chart or another graphic that shows the information you found.

Word Relationships

Focus Skill

How many different meanings for the word *back* can you think of? The English language has many multiple-meaning words, like *back*. Homophones and homographs are other kinds of multiple-meaning words. Here are some clues to help you understand the special relationships of these words.

Multiple-Meaning Words		
Homophones	**Homographs**	**Other Multiple-Meaning Words**
past, passed see, sea one, won by, buy	*live* [līv] *adj.* having life *live* [liv] *v.* to make one's home *tear* [tir] *n.* a drop that comes from the eye when crying *tear* [târ] *v.* to rip	*right*—"a direction" or "correct" *run*—"to go faster than walking" or "a tear in material"
Clue: The spelling of the word tells you the correct meaning. You can use a dictionary to confirm the meaning.	Clue: Use context, or the way the word is used in a sentence, to figure out the correct pronunciation and meaning.	Clue: Use context, or the words and sentences surrounding the word, to figure out the correct meaning.

**Visit *The Learning Site!*
www.harcourtschool.com**

See *Skills* and *Activities*

Test Prep
Word Relationships

> One morning Little Cave Girl went out to gather some berries. She took her <u>bow</u> and arrows, just in case. Soon she found a bush covered with ripe, red berries. She filled her bowl with berries. On the way home, she met a baby dinosaur. She gave him some of the berries. He <u>ate</u> them and asked for more. By the time Little Cave Girl got home, she had only <u>eight</u> berries in the bowl for her breakfast.

1. **Which pronunciation is correct for the word <u>bow</u> in this paragraph?**

   A rhymes with <u>cow</u>

   B rhymes with <u>go</u>

   C rhymes with <u>too</u>

   D rhymes with <u>saw</u>

   Tip

   Think about what the word means in the paragraph to help you choose the correct pronunciation.

2. **How are the words <u>ate</u> and <u>eight</u> related?**

   F They are synonyms.

   G They are antonyms, or opposites.

   H They are homophones.

   J They are homographs.

   Tip

   Compare the two words. Think about their meanings and about how they are spelled and pronounced.

▲ Rosie, a Visiting
Dog's Story

Vocabulary Power

firm

confident

comfortable

equipment

program

appointment

approach

Helping others is important. One town made up this flyer to find someone who wants to help others by coaching a baseball team.

WANTED:
YOUTH BASEBALL COACH

Our town needs a baseball coach to work with young players. We're looking for someone who

- can be **firm** and help players follow rules.
- is **confident** and knows that he or she can do the job.
- feels **comfortable** and at ease with people of all ages.
- can transport **equipment**, such as balls, bats, and bases.
- has time to prepare a youth **program** by planning practices and games.
- enjoys young people and baseball!

Are you the person we're looking for? If you think you are, call the Town Hall for an **appointment**, and we'll set a time to meet with you. Or you can **approach** any member of the committee. Come up to us if you see us on the street, and tell us why you'd like to be our new coach!

Vocabulary–Writing CONNECTION

Choose a sport that you enjoy. List at least five pieces of **equipment** that you can use to play the sport.

257

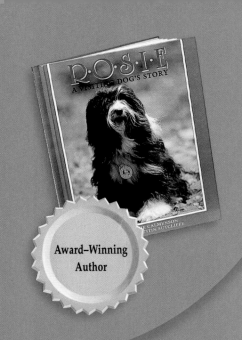

Genre

Personal Narrative

A personal narrative tells a true story about something important to the author.

In this selection, look for

- first-person point of view.

- the author's personal thoughts and feelings.

ROSIE,
A VISITING DOG'S STORY

by Stephanie Calmenson
photographs by Justin Sutcliffe

This is Rosie, my dog. She loves to play fetch. She will roll over to have her belly rubbed. And she will lick you on the nose if you are her friend.

Rosie is like many other dogs—maybe even like your dog. But in one way, Rosie is special.

Rosie is a working dog. Here she is in her uniform. Her red harness and special badges say to everyone, *I am a visiting dog.* A visiting dog's job is to cheer up people who are sad, or sick, or lonely.

Rosie was not always a visiting dog. She had to be trained for her work.

This is how Rosie looked when she was a puppy. You could see her eyes! Rosie the puppy would not have been a good visiting dog. She was too wild and silly.

Rosie liked to snoop. Rosie left puddles in all the wrong places. Rosie chewed everything in sight!

But even as a puppy Rosie was gentle and friendly. And she was a good listener. I knew that Rosie would make a good visiting dog someday.

We started Rosie's training at puppy kindergarten. Robin Kovary was our teacher. She taught me how to teach Rosie.

Robin was firm but always gentle. That was important because Rosie had to trust people. She had to be confident that no one would harm her. Rosie also needed to keep her independent spirit. She might have to make a decision on her own while working one day.

Rosie liked school. She learned her lessons fast.

Rosie, sit. Good dog!

Rosie, down. Good dog!

Rosie, stay. Good dog!

Rosie, come. Good dog!

At home, I tried to prepare Rosie for her work. First, it was important for Rosie to be a happy dog. After all, a sad dog could not cheer anyone up. So we played a lot of games. Her favorites were fetch and "catch-me-if-you-can."

Rosie would also have to get along with other dogs in case she had to work alongside them. So she got plenty of time to play with her friends.

A good visiting dog has to be comfortable with all kinds of people. I introduced Rosie to as many different people as I could.

On one street Rosie would sit quietly with an elderly person.

On the next street she would run and play with a child.

Rosie always had good sense. If a person wanted to play, Rosie played. If a person seemed shy, Rosie would lie down and wait for the person to come to her.

263

Rosie was ready to join a visiting dog program at the ASPCA[1] when she was two years old. Her real training was about to begin.

Our teacher was Micky Niego. In the class there were big dogs and small dogs, short-haired and long-haired dogs, pedigrees and mixed breeds.

All the dogs had two things in common: They were friendly and they were happy to work.

Micky began the class by having the dogs practice their basic obedience skills: Sit, down, stay, come. Then Micky added new skills.

[1]ASPCA: American Society for the Prevention of Cruelty to Animals

Rosie learned to "Go say hello." This means that Rosie will not approach a person until she is told that the person is ready to greet her.

She learned the "Don't touch" command. When Rosie hears it she will not touch food or anything else until she hears, "Okay, take it!" It is important for Rosie never to be rude and grab from a person.

The people Rosie would visit might be using wheelchairs and walkers. So Rosie had to be comfortable with all kinds of equipment.

Rosie also had to get used to being handled in different ways. A young child might pull her tail or her long hair, not knowing any better.

An elderly or ill person might pet her too roughly by mistake.

Rosie had to be patient and gentle even at times like these.

Rosie also had to be a good traveler. To get to work, Rosie might need to ride on a train, a bus, or even an airplane. Rosie was given a special travel pass, which allows her to ride with me.

We took many trips together. Rosie learned to be a quiet, well-mannered traveler. And, of course, she made lots of friends.

After four months of training, Rosie and her classmates were tested. Rosie went into a room with volunteers. The volunteers behaved the way the people Rosie would visit might behave.

A little girl with tubes was on a bed. Rosie did not nip at the tubes the way she would have when she was a puppy. Rosie lay quietly by the little girl's side.

A woman dropped a walker in front of Rosie. Rosie did not bark or snap or act fearful. She calmly stepped out of the way.

There were many tests. Rosie passed them all with flying colors!

A few weeks later, Rosie's badges came in the mail. It was time for our first visit. We were invited to a children's hospital.

Before we went, I took Rosie to her vet, Dr. Jimmy Corrao, for a checkup. A visiting dog has to be healthy.

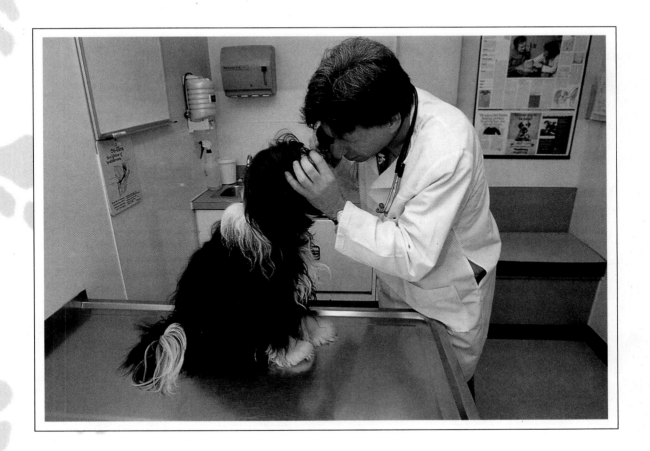

Then I gave Rosie a bath in a special shampoo that made her feel soft and smell sweet.

On the day of our visit, I packed water for Rosie to drink, a soft brush in case someone wanted to groom her, a ball so she could play, and Cheerios to eat.

When we went outside, Rosie had on her red harness, her badges, and a big red bow. I could see that Rosie was proud. She held her head up high.

At the children's hospital, David James, the program director, was waiting for us. I introduced myself and then Rosie.

"Rosie, sit. Paw, please," I said.

Rosie gave Mr. James her paw.

"Hello, Rosie," said Mr. James. "I have some friends I want you to meet. Follow me."

Rosie made a lot of new friends that day. Nina is in a wheelchair because she cannot use her legs. But she has a great throwing arm.

"Rosie, fetch!" she called. Nina threw the ball way across the room. Lucky Rosie! She loves to fetch.

Peter, who is blind, carefully brushed Rosie's long coat.

"Rosie would like to say thank you," I told him.

I turned to Rosie and said, "Speak!" Rosie barked twice to thank Peter for grooming her so well.

In the next room we met Alexander. Alexander was by himself because he was too sick that day to play with other children. Rosie loved Alexander right away.

The first thing she did was roll over on her back, so Alexander could rub her belly. That made Alexander laugh.

"Rosie looks like a shaggy rug!" he said.

Then Alexander lay down beside Rosie and they napped together awhile.

When they woke up, they shared some Cheerios. I told Alexander how to keep Rosie from grabbing them.

"Rosie, don't touch!" said Alexander.

Rosie turned her head away.

"Okay, take them!" Alexander said.

Rosie ate the Cheerios from Alexander's hand. Then she licked Alexander on the cheek and got a big hug in return.

A few weeks later a call came from The Village Nursing Home asking if Rosie would like to come and visit. We set up an appointment for the next afternoon.

Bea was the first person we met. Bea cannot use her arms or legs, and she has no feeling in them. Bea likes to watch Rosie and to feel Rosie's soft fur against her face.

Then we met Thomas. Thomas was in a wheelchair. Rosie made herself at home in his lap.

"She's cuddly, just like my grandson!" said Thomas.

Down the hall, we heard a woman crying.

"I have so many problems," she said.

"Maybe you'll feel better if you tell them to Rosie," I suggested. "Rosie is a very good listener."

"Rosie?" she asked. She wiped away her tears and started to smile. "My name is Rosie, too!"

The two Rosies had a good visit. Then Linda, a nurse, asked us to look in on Bill down the hall.

"Don't worry if he won't talk to you. He hasn't spoken to anyone in weeks. And he hardly eats. I think he's very lonely," she explained.

I brought Rosie to Bill's room.

"Would you like a visitor?" I asked.

Bill looked at Rosie, then turned away. But then he turned back. For a few minutes he just stared.

Finally he asked in a very quiet voice, "How can the little dog see?"

I told Bill how Rosie's long lashes hold up her hair to let her see through. Suddenly Bill was ready to visit. He had a lot to say about dogs with long hair, and the dog he had when he was a child, and how he wished he had his dog for company now.

I told Bill that Rosie would come visit him again soon. By the time we left, Bill did not seem so lonely anymore. He was saying to Linda, "My dog, Harley, loved to eat cherry Jell-O. Are we having Jell-O for dessert tonight?"

Linda was so happy, she said, "You will have Jell-O if I have to make it for you myself!"

When we left the nursing home, Rosie's tail was way up high and wagging. I offered her a drink of cool water. Then I lifted up her hair to look in her eyes. They were clear and bright.

"Rosie, you are a very good visiting dog," I said. "You are a very good friend."

Think and Respond

1. What makes Rosie a good visiting dog?

2. What do the captions under the pictures on page 262 tell you?

3. Why is it important for Rosie not to **approach** someone until the person is **comfortable** with her?

4. What might people learn from Rosie about being a good friend?

5. How did you use reading strategies to help you understand this selection? Give one example.

Author and Her Dog Cheer Many

Stephanie Calmenson is the author of many books for children. She is also the owner of a Tibetan terrier named Rosie. She has trained Rosie to visit sick or lonely people in hospitals and nursing homes in New York City.

When asked why she brings Rosie on these visits, Stephanie Calmenson said, "Ever since I was a little girl living in Brooklyn, I wanted a dog, but I couldn't have one. When I grew up, I got Rosie. She turned out to be so sweet, I wanted to share her with as many people as I could. That is why we joined the visiting dog program."

Before she became a writer, Stephanie Calmenson was a teacher and then an editor for a children's book publisher. The first story she wrote was printed in a magazine. Many people liked her story. Their praise encouraged her to keep on writing.

Visit *The Learning Site!*
www.harcourtschool.com

Making Connections

Compare Texts

1. Why do you think "Rosie, a Visiting Dog's Story" is included in a theme about people and animals working as a team?

2. Where in this selection could the author have used subheadings to divide the text? What subheadings would you use?

3. Name a fiction story you know that has a dog as a main character. In what ways is Rosie like the dog in the story? In what ways is she different?

4. Would Rosie want to be a house pet now that she's become a visiting dog? Why or why not?

5. Who in your community can provide information on training visiting dogs?

Write a Description

Think of a dog or another pet that you know and like. Write a paragraph to help readers form a picture of the pet in their minds. Tell how the pet looks, feels, and sounds. Explain why the pet is special. Use vivid words and phrases. Jot them down in a web like this one.

Writing CONNECTION

Pet Description

Give an Oral Report

Rosie is trained by the ASPCA to be a visiting dog. Use the telephone directory or the Internet to find another organization that trains animals to help in other ways. For example, animals may be trained to work with police officers or to help people who are challenged. Take notes, and prepare an oral report to present to your classmates.

Social Studies CONNECTION

✓ Name of organization
✓ How to contact
✓ Type of animal
✓ What the animals do

Take a Survey

Make a survey that asks your classmates about their pets. You might ask what kinds of pets they have and how many, what care the pets require, or how much time they spend playing with their pets. Then prepare a written report and a chart or graph to display your survey results.

Math CONNECTION

Decode Long Words

When you come upon a long word in your reading, think about how to break it into smaller parts. Here are the steps you can take to decode long words.

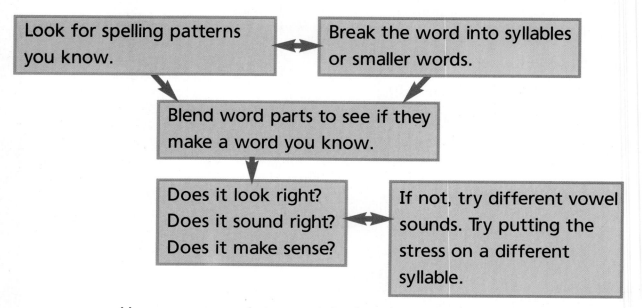

Look for spelling patterns you know. ↔ Break the word into syllables or smaller words.

Blend word parts to see if they make a word you know.

Does it look right? Does it sound right? Does it make sense? ↔ If not, try different vowel sounds. Try putting the stress on a different syllable.

Here are some long words that have been divided into smaller parts. Can you read them?

kin · der · gar · ten

in · de · pen · dent

wheel · chairs

Test Prep
Decode Long Words

▶ **Read the passage. Then answer the questions.**

> Dogs of all sizes are <u>intelligent</u> animals. Their cleverness has proved to be of great benefit to humans. For example, huge St. Bernard dogs have rescued about 2,000 people from the dangerous mountains in the Alps. They help clear <u>pathways</u> through the snow with their broad chests.

1. **What spelling pattern helps you say the last syllable of the word <u>intelligent</u>?**

   A consonant-vowel-consonant-<u>e</u>

   B <u>g</u> followed by <u>e</u> or <u>i</u> has the soft sound /j/

   C the letter pattern <u>lig</u>

   D vowel-consonant spelling: <u>-in</u>

Tip

Find the letters that make up the last syllable. Think of other words you know with that spelling pattern.

2. **Which strategy best helps you read the word <u>pathways</u>?**

   F syllable patterns

   G spelling patterns

   H changing the syllable stressed

   J looking for smaller words

Tip

Read each answer choice. Look back at the word to see which choice is most helpful.

Friends to Grow with

CONTENTS

▲ The Stories
Julian Tells

| mustache |
| fastened |
| beyond |
| cartwheel |
| seriously |
| collection |

Vocabulary Power

In "The Stories Julian Tells," Julian wishes he had a friend his own age. Look at these pictures that show some friends having fun.

How do you like my **mustache**? I stuck some fake fur between my nose and lip to look like hair. My friends couldn't figure out how I got it to stick. I **fastened** it with tape that's sticky on both sides.

Look past the bushes. Do you see me there, **beyond** them? My friends didn't see me. I sneaked up and scared them!

I couldn't do a **cartwheel** until my friends showed me how. Now we all try to turn sideways on our hands and not fall over.

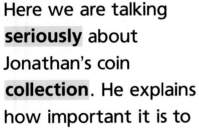

Here we are talking **seriously** about Jonathan's coin **collection**. He explains how important it is to protect the coins. He has coins from all over the world. The longer he has them, the more valuable they become.

Vocabulary–Writing CONNECTION

Tell what you do when you want your friends to take you **seriously**. Do you look or dress a certain way? Write four senten̶c̶e̶s̶ ̶t̶o̶ ̶d̶e̶s̶c̶r̶ibe what you̶ ̶ what̶

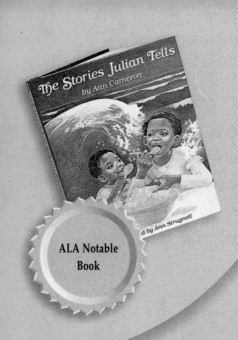

ALA Notable Book

Genre

Realistic Fiction

Realistic fiction tells about characters and events that are like people and events in real life.

In this selection, look for

- **a story that is told by a main character.**

- **the main character's thoughts and f̶e̶e̶l̶i̶n̶g̶s̶.**

THE STORIES JULIAN TELLS

by Ann Cameron

illustrated by Cornelius Van Wright
and Ying-Hwa Hu

Gloria, Who Might Be My Best Friend

If you have a girl for a friend, people find out and tease you. That's why I didn't want a girl for a friend — not until this summer, when I met Gloria.

It happened one afternoon when I was walking down the street by myself. My mother was visiting a friend of hers, and Huey was visiting a friend of his. Huey's friend is five and so I think he is too young to play with. And there aren't any kids just my age. I was walking down the street feeling lonely.

A block from our house I saw a moving van in front of a brown house, and men were carrying in chairs and tables and bookcases and boxes full of I don't know what. I watched for a while, and suddenly I heard a voice right behind me.

"Who are you?"

I turned around and there was a girl in a yellow dress. She looked the same age as me. She had curly hair that was braided into two pigtails with red ribbons at the ends.

"I'm Julian," I said. "Who are you?"

"I'm Gloria," she said. "I come from Newport. Do you know where Newport is?"

I wasn't sure, but I didn't tell Gloria. "It's a town on the ocean," I said.

"Right," Gloria said. "Can you turn a cartwheel?"

She turned sideways herself and did two cartwheels on the grass.

I had never tried a cartwheel before, but I tried to copy Gloria. My hands went down in the grass, my feet went up in the air, and—I fell over.

I looked at Gloria to see if she was laughing at me. If she was laughing at me, I was going to go home and forget about her.

But she just looked at me very seriously and said, "It takes practice," and then I liked her.

"I know where there's a bird's nest in your yard," I said.

"Really?" Gloria said. "There weren't any trees in the yard, or any birds, where I lived before."

I showed her where a robin lives and has eggs. Gloria stood up on a branch and looked in. The eggs were small and pale blue. The mother robin squawked at us, and she and the father robin flew around our heads.

"They want us to go away," Gloria said. She got down from the branch, and we went around to the front of the house and watched the moving men carry two rugs and a mirror inside.

"Would you like to come over to my house?" I said.

"All right," Gloria said, "if it is all right with my mother." She ran in the house and asked.

It was all right, so Gloria and I went to my house, and I showed her my room and my games and my rock collection, and then I made strawberry Kool-Aid and we sat at the kitchen table and drank it.

"You have a red mustache on your mouth," Gloria said.

"You have a red mustache on your mouth, too," I said.

Gloria giggled, and we licked off the mustaches with our tongues.

"I wish you'd live here a long time," I told Gloria.

Gloria said, "I wish I would too."

"I know the best way to make wishes," Gloria said.

"What's that?" I asked.

"First you make a kite. Do you know how to make one?"

"Yes," I said, "I know how." I know how to make good kites because my father taught me. We make them out of two crossed sticks and folded newspaper.

"All right," Gloria said, "that's the first part of making wishes that come true. So let's make a kite."

We went out into the garage and spread out sticks and newspaper and made a kite. I fastened on the kite string and went to the closet and got rags for the tail.

"Do you have some paper and two pencils?" Gloria asked. "Because now we make the wishes."

I didn't know what she was planning, but I went in the
house and got pencils and paper.

"All right," Gloria said. "Every wish you want to have come
true you write on a long thin piece of paper. You don't tell me
your wishes, and I don't tell you mine. If you tell, your wishes
don't come true. Also, if you look at the other person's wishes,
your wishes don't come true."

Gloria sat down on the garage floor again and started
writing her wishes. I wanted to see what they were — but
I went to the other side of the garage and wrote my own
wishes instead. I wrote:

1. I wish I could see the catalog cats.

2. I wish the fig tree would be the tallest in town.

3. I wish I'd be a great soccer player.

4. I wish I could ride in an airplane.

5. I wish Gloria would stay here and be my best friend.

I folded my five wishes in my fist and went over to Gloria.

"How many wishes did you make?" Gloria asked.

"Five," I said. "How many did you make?"

"Two," Gloria said.

I wondered what they were.

"Now we put the wishes on the tail of the kite," Gloria said. "Every time we tie one piece of rag on the tail, we fasten a wish in the knot. You can put yours in first."

I fastened mine in, and then Gloria fastened in hers, and we carried the kite into the yard.

"You hold the tail," I told Gloria, "and I'll pull."

We ran through the back yard with the kite, passed the garden and the fig tree, and went into the open field beyond our yard.

The kite started to rise. The tail jerked heavily like a long white snake. In a minute the kite passed the roof of my house and was climbing toward the sun.

We stood in the open field, looking up at it. I was wishing I would get my wishes.

"I know it's going to work!" Gloria said.

"How do you know?"

"When we take the kite down," Gloria told me, "there shouldn't be one wish in the tail. When the wind takes all your wishes, that's when you know it's going to work." The kite stayed up for a long time. We both held the string.

The kite looked like a tiny black spot in the sun, and my neck got stiff from looking at it.

"Shall we pull it in?" I asked.

"All right," Gloria said.

We drew the string in more and more until, like a tired bird, the kite fell at our feet.

We looked at the tail. All our wishes were gone. Probably they were still flying higher and higher in the wind.

Maybe I would see the catalog cats and get to be a good soccer player and have a ride in an airplane and the tallest fig tree in town. And Gloria would be my best friend.

"Gloria," I said, "did you wish we would be friends?"

"You're not supposed to ask me that!" Gloria said.

"I'm sorry," I answered. But inside I was smiling. I guessed one thing Gloria wished for. I was pretty sure we would be friends.

THINK AND RESPOND

1 Why is "Gloria, Who Might Be My Best Friend" a good title for this story?

2 If you made a video of this story, what three places would you need to show?

3 Do you think Julian will be less lonely now that he knows Gloria? Give reasons for your answer.

4 Julian has a rock **collection**. What kind of collection would you like to have? Explain your reasons.

5 Give an example to show how you used a reading strategy to understand something in the story.

Meet the Author
Ann Cameron

Question: Who was your best friend when you were growing up?

Ann Cameron: My best friend was a boy named Bradley. I got teased about him because we were together a lot.

Question: So a boy was your best friend, and you were teased about this. Why did you decide to have Gloria as Julian's best friend?

Ann Cameron: I had a friend from South Africa, Julian, who told me about his childhood—the kite that he flew; his brother, Huey; and his best friend, Gloria. I thought it was neat that Julian's best friend had been a girl. I never thought of leaving her out of the stories.

Question: What do you hope children will find out from this story?

Ann Cameron: I think it's VERY important for people to have good friends. I hope children will reach out and find the happiness that comes with friendship.

Ann Cameron

Visit _The Learning Site!_
www.harcourtschool.com

298

Meet the Illustrators
Cornelius Van Wright and Ying-Hwa Hu

Question: How long have you been working as a team?

Ying-Hwa Hu: We have been working together since 1989.

Question: How many projects have you worked on?

Ying-Hwa Hu: We have done fifteen picture books together. We have both worked on other books separately.

Question: How do you split up the work on a book you illustrate together?

Cornelius Van Wright: Usually I work out with the publisher what will be pictured on each page. Together, Ying-Hwa and I work on the look of the people. Both of us do some of the drawing. We try to work with each other's strengths. When we paint, one starts and passes it to the other.

Making Connections

Compare Texts

1 How does "The Stories Julian Tells" fit the theme Friends to Grow With?

2 What does Gloria do to change Julian's mind about having a girl for a friend?

3 Compare the look on Julian's face on page 288 with how he looks on page 294. What do these pictures show you?

4 Think of two friends you know that are most like Julian and Gloria. Explain how the two people are similar to the story characters.

5 What do you think Julian will do if people tease him about having a girl for a friend?

Write Instructions

HOW TO

Steps to follow:
1. _____
2. _____
3. _____
4. _____
5. _____

In the story, Julian says he knows how to make good kites because his father taught him. Think of something you know how to do well—such as making a sandwich, setting a table, or making a greeting card. Write instructions that tell a younger student how to do it. Use a graphic like the one here to organize your instructions. Add as many steps as you need.

Writing
CONNECTION

Make a Booklet

Julian shows Gloria a robin's nest in her yard. Choose a bird that you have seen near your home or school. Do research to find out interesting facts about it. You might use a field guide, an encyclopedia, or other sources. Then create a booklet about the bird. Make a cover and draw some illustrations for your booklet.

Science
CONNECTION

Experiment with Shapes

Look at the picture of Julian and Gloria's kite on page 284. Do you see the triangle shapes in the kite? Follow these directions to learn more about triangles.

- Draw the shape of a kite and use a ruler to draw the crossed lines.
- Which of the triangles have the same shape and size?
- Cut your kite into four triangles.
- Exchange with a classmate two triangles that are not the same size and shape.
- Try to use the new set of triangles to put your kite back together.
- Discuss what happens with a classmate.

Math
CONNECTION

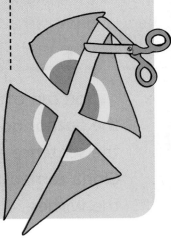

Sequence

In "The Stories Julian Tells," Julian and Gloria's friendship becomes stronger as they spend time together. To help you understand the time that passes during the story, the author uses signal words.

This chart uses examples from the story to explain how signal words are clues to the **sequence** of events.

Example	Signal Word Clue	Other Clues
That's why I didn't want a girl for a friend—not until this <u>summer</u>, when I met Gloria.	time-of-year clue	spring, fall, winter, holidays, months
It happened one <u>afternoon</u> when I was walking down the street by myself.	part-of-day clue	sunrise, morning, noon, evening, night, sunset
I fastened mine in, and <u>then</u> Gloria fastened in hers, and we carried the kite into the yard.	time-order word	after, before, later, soon, now, first, next, last

You can often tell the sequence of events even when the author does not use signal words. For example, in the sentence about the kite, you know that Julian and Gloria carried the kite into the yard *after* they fastened the wishes.

**Visit *The Learning Site!*
www.harcourtschool.com**

See *Skills* and *Activities*

302

Test Prep

Sequence

▶ **Events in stories happen in a certain order, or sequence. Here is a passage from a story. Read the passage. Then do numbers 1 and 2.**

> Today, Isabel decided, she would introduce herself. A week ago, a new family had moved into the yellow house down the street. Isabel had seen a boy who looked about her age. Since then it had rained every day, but now the sun was out at last.

1. **Which event happened first?**

   A Isabel decided to introduce herself.

   B The sun came out.

   C A new family moved into the yellow house.

   D Isabel saw a boy who looked about her age.

Tip

Use time-order clues that the author gives to help you decide when events happened.

2. **When did the rain begin?**

   F before the new family moved in

   G before Isabel first saw the boy

   H after the new family moved in

   J the day Isabel decided to introduce herself

Tip

Read and think about each choice. Rule out incorrect choices.

perform

recite

gym

roam

prefer

enjoying

billions

Vocabulary Power

"**T**he Talent Show" tells about students taking part in a show at their school. How do you have fun at school? Tyler made a list of the things he likes best about third grade.

**The Five Best Things About
Third Grade So Far
by Tyler**

1. I got to **perform** in our class play, <u>Goldilocks and the Three Bears</u>. I played the part of Papa Bear. I was able to **recite** my part from memory without forgetting any lines.

2. I like playing soccer in the **gym**. We're lucky to have such a large room in our school where we can **roam** around and play games. Sometimes, I just wander from one game to another.

3. This year I found out that sometimes I **prefer** reading to playing games. Before this, I always liked playing games better.

4. I am **enjoying** math more because I understand it better. Now I'm having a good time doing my math.

5. I learned that although there are **billions** of people in the world — more than you could ever count — there is only one ME!

Vocabulary-Writing
CONNECTION

Write two short paragraphs. First, describe the things you **prefer** to do with your family. Second, describe what you **prefer** to do with your friends.

Genre

Realistic Fiction

Realistic fiction tells about characters and events that are like people and events in real life.

In this selection, look for

- **characters that are like people you know and events that could really happen.**

- **a setting that could be a real place.**

Ms. Babbitt came to school one morning wearing her smiley face earrings, the ones that mean something special is going to happen. Kelsey asked her why she was wearing them. But Ms. Babbitt said she wouldn't tell till the end of the day.

Right before dismissal Ms. Babbitt said, "Boys and girls, I have something special to announce. Two weeks from today this class is going to have a talent show. It'll be in the gym, and all the first, second, and third graders will come to see it. We won't have winners. We won't have prizes. It's just going to be for fun.

Talent Show

by Susan Wojciechowski ★ illustrated by Laura Ovresat

You may perform anything you'd like—a poem, a song, a joke, a dance. Are there any questions?"

Carol Ann asked, "Can we wear costumes?"

"You may wear costumes or not, whichever you prefer."

Steven asked, "Can we do stuff in groups?"

"You may perform alone or in groups."

Pam asked, "If we say a poem, do we have to rememberize it, or can we read it off a paper?"

"I think it would be much more effective if you memorized it."

Leo asked, "Can I have my dog in my act?"

"You may, but someone must bring the dog at the time of the show. It may not roam around our classroom all day distracting the class."

Wendy, who's shy and talks so quietly you can hardly hear her, asked, "Do we have to do something?"

"No one has to be in the show, but I think those of you who choose to be a part of it will have lots of fun."

The dismissal bell rang and we all ran for the buses, talking about the talent show.

That night, Carol Ann called me on the phone. "Beany, I have the greatest idea for the talent show. You and I are going to recite a poem together. I wrote a poem that has lines for two people to say. It's about bees—a queen bee and a worker bee. It'll be the best act in the whole show. If they gave awards, this act would win first place. We'll practice every day after school. My mother will make the costumes. You'll be the worker bee and I'll be the queen bee."

"Why do you get to be the queen?" I asked.

"Because I have curly hair, silly. Don't you know anything?"

The next day Carol Ann gave me a copy of the poem. We practiced at her house after school. Carol Ann stretched out on big pillows to say her lines. I had to stand holding a mop and a pail. Carol Ann said those were props and they made us look our parts.

I didn't want to hold a pail and mop while Carol Ann lay on pillows, but I didn't complain because, number one, Carol Ann is very bossy and I'm a tiny bit scared of her and, number two, I didn't have any better ideas for an act.

The day after that we practiced at my house. Carol Ann wore a crown. I didn't.

On Saturday Carol Ann decided I should say my lines in a low, growly voice like a worker who is tired and she should say her lines soft and tinkly like a queen.

On Monday Carol Ann showed me pictures she drew of the costumes. Carol Ann's had a gold ruffled ballerina skirt. Mine had a big black-and-yellow-striped T-shirt and black tights.

Bee Poem

A week before the show Carol Ann said, "Let's talk about all the things that might go wrong."

"Let's not," I said.

Carol Ann ignored that and started to list them: "I'm worried you might forget your lines, or drop your mop, or get a run in your tights, or trip over your pail, or get the hiccups, or sneeze."

That's when I started to worry. I worried that I would spit when I talked. I worried that my antennae would fall down over my face. I worried that instead of saying, "I feed the queen and build the hive," I would say, "I feed the hive and build the queen."

Every night at supper I said my lines to my family. Every night in bed I bit my nails thinking about doing the bee poem.

One night as I was repeating, "I feed the queen and build the hive," over and over during supper, my dad said, "Beany, relax. You're supposed to be enjoying this talent show."

"I know. Ms. Babbitt even said the show was for fun. But I'm not having any. I know I'll do something wrong and Carol Ann will be mad at me."

"Then why are you doing an act with her?" my brother asked.

"It just sort of happened. Besides, I don't have any better ideas."

"How about doing the cartwheels you just learned in gymnastics class?" my mother asked. "Your teacher said you do them really well."

"Carol Ann wouldn't like that. She's got everything all figured out for us."

That night as I lay in bed biting my nails, my dad tiptoed into my room.

"Are you awake?" he whispered.

"I can't sleep," I said. "I'm thinking about the bee poem."

"I want to show you something wonderful," Dad said. He swung me and Jingle Bell onto his back and carried us down the stairs and out the front door. There were two sleeping bags spread out on the driveway. Jingle Bell and I lay on top of one of them and Dad lay on the other.

"Look at the sky," he said. "I don't think I've ever seen it so beautiful. I wanted to share it with you."

Dad was right. The sky looked like black ink. The stars looked like white polka dots.

"How many stars are there?" I asked my dad.

"Billions," he answered.

"I mean, what's the exact number?"

"That's a mystery."

"I'm going to count them," I decided. So I picked a spot to start at and tried to keep track of which stars I had counted and which ones were left. When I got to twenty-seven, I got mixed up and had to start over. This time I got to thirty-two before I got mixed up again. I started a third time.

Dad stopped me. "You know something, Beany? I don't think you should count the stars. There are some things in life that are just meant to be enjoyed."

"You mean like a dish of double chocolate ice cream with colored sprinkles and whipped cream on top?" I asked.

"Yes," he said, "and like a sausage, pepperoni, and onion pizza."

"And like kittens," I added.

"Right. And like Beethoven's Fifth Symphony."

"And like a starry, starry night, Daddy?"

"Yes, like a starry, starry night."

We looked up at the sky for a while. Then my dad asked, "Do you know what else should just be enjoyed?"

"What?"

"A talent show."

He reached over to my sleeping bag and squeezed my hand. We lay there looking up at the stars for a long time. Not counting them. Just enjoying them.

The next day on the bus ride to school I took a deep breath and said to Carol Ann, "I don't want to do the bee poem. I want to do cartwheels across the gym floor."

"Why?" she asked.

"Because cartwheels are fun."

"What would you wear?"

"Shorts and a T-shirt."

"What kind of music would you have?"

"No music."

"How many cartwheels would you do?"

"As many as it takes."

"What if you fall?"

"I'll get up and keep going."

"What if you do a cartwheel into Kevin Gates?"

"Carol Ann, quit it," I said. "I'm doing cartwheels no matter what you say." Then I gave her back the paper with my bee poem lines.

On Friday our class put on the best talent show in the whole world. For his talent, Boomer Fenton showed his birthmark in the shape of a dog's face. Kelsey played "Twinkle, Twinkle, Little Star" on her violin. Leo tried to get his dog to roll over, but the dog ran under Ms. Babbitt's chair and wouldn't come out for the rest of the show. Carol Ann and Wendy did the bee poem. Carol Ann's crown fell off right in the middle of it.

For my talent, I did cartwheels from one end of the gym to the other. It was fun.

Think and Respond

1. Why does Beany change her mind about being in the talent show with Carol Ann?

2. What is Beany's father like? How do you know?

3. How does Beany show courage in this story?

4. If your class put on a talent show, what kind of act would you **perform**?

5. Give an example of a reading strategy you used as you read this story.

Meet the Author
Susan Wojciechowski

A few years ago Susan Wojciechowski had the flu. While she was lying in bed, the idea for a story character, Beany, popped into her head. "Beany just stayed there, and by the time I was well, the stories were written," she said.

Susan Wojciechowski wasn't always a writer. First, she was a school teacher. Later, she worked as a school librarian. She is also the mother of three children.

Her books include stories for teenagers as well as picture books for young readers. She hopes that her readers see her characters as real people and that they see a little of themselves in Beany.

The Last Case of the I.C. Detective Agency

by Carol M. Harris   **illustrated by Linda Helton**

"Hey!" Ivan's little brother, Ben, yelled. "The new people are pulling up. I see a kid."

Ivan didn't care if twenty kids moved into Apartment 2A where his friend Charlie used to live. Nobody could replace Charlie. It was Charlie who had started the I.C. Detective Agency (*I* for Ivan, *C* for Charlie). It was Charlie who had thought of all the good ideas and found all the good cases. Now that he had moved away, there would be no detective agency, no cases, and no fun.

For two whole days Ivan managed to avoid the new kid in 2A. "Her name is Ursula, and she's going to be in your class," his little brother told him. "She says she wants to be friends with you."

Ivan didn't want to be friends with her. But one day she came right up to him while he was sitting on the front steps, and she said, "Hi. Ben told me you have a detective agency."

"Well, I don't," Ivan mumbled. He started to leave.

"That's too bad," she said with a frown. "I need a detective."

He stared at her. "What for?"

"Why should I tell you if you're not a detective? I'll figure it out myself." She started down the stairs.

"Wait! Figure what out?"

She took a crumpled paper out of her pocket and shoved it at him. "What does this mean?"

Ivan smoothed out the paper and read the words printed on it:

"Where did this come from?" he asked, staring at Ursula.

"It was between the window and the screen in my bedroom," she answered. "Spooky, huh? It looks like code. I think spies lived in our apartment before we moved in."

"Charlie lived there, dopey," Ivan said.

"Maybe he was a spy."

"He wasn't a spy, dopey. He was my partner in the I.C. Detective Agency."

"Well, he couldn't have been a very good detective if he didn't see this note," Ursula said, pulling it away from him. "And stop calling me 'dopey'!"

"I'm sorry," Ivan said quickly. "I'll help you."

He knew it wouldn't be the same as working on a case with Charlie, but it was better than nothing.

"Do you want to take a look at the crime scene?" Ursula asked.

Ivan's eyes widened. She knew detective talk.

It was strange seeing Ursula's mother instead of Charlie's in Apartment 2A, and it was even stranger to be working on a case in the room where he and his friend had solved so many mysteries together. Ursula pointed out the spot where she'd found the note, then sat down at her desk.

"Here," she said, handing Ivan a paper and pencil. "Let's get to work."

"We have to find the code breaker," Ivan said, bending his head over the paper. "1234567 has to be it. We've got to figure out what that word is."

"You mean the numbers stand for letters?" Ursula asked.

"Sure. At least that's how most codes work," he explained. "They substitute a number for each letter of the alphabet, like 1 for *A* and 2 for *B*, and 3 for *C*. Charlie and I used that code sometimes."

But when Ivan and Ursula tried it on the note, it didn't work. "It doesn't make sense," said Ursula, looking over his shoulder.

"I know." Ivan scratched his head. "I wish Charlie were here," he muttered. "We'd work it out in no time."

500K UND74 T27 4UG. 1234567
E00K UNDGD TBG DUG. ABCDEFG

Ursula looked up. "Hey!" she said suddenly. "Was this Charlie's room?"

"Yeah. So?"

She didn't answer but started scribbling furiously. "That's it," she yelled. Then she ran to each corner of the room and tugged at the edges of the rug.

Ivan watched with a puzzled expression as she bent down and pulled up a loose corner of the rug.

"Bingo!" Triumphantly she held up a second note. She read it quickly. Dancing across the room, she handed the first note to Ivan. "Read this," she ordered.

500K UND74 T27 4UG. 1234567
E00K UNDGD TBG DUG. ABCDEFG
LOOK UNDER THE RUG. CHARLIE

"Charlie?" Ivan wrinkled his forehead.

"Your friend Charlie left that note," Ursula said, laughing. "He used his own name for the code breaker."

"I don't believe it," Ivan said.

She handed him the second note. "Read it out loud."

Ivan read:

TO WHOEVER FINDS THIS NOTE:

You passed the test. You cracked the code. Ask Ivan if you can be in the I.C. Detective Agency. He needs a new partner.

Charlie (code breaker 1234567)

"Boy, leave it to Charlie to do something like this!" Ivan said.

"Well?" Ursula asked. "Can I be in the I.C. Detective Agency?"

Ivan shook his head. "No."

She frowned. "But didn't Charlie's note say . . ."

Ivan laughed. "I think we need a new name," he said. "How about the I.C.U. Detective Agency?"

"I get it," Ursula said. "*I* for Ivan, *C* for Charlie, and *U* for Ursula."

"Right! You're a great detective!"

"I know," she said with a grin. "I think our first case should be to send a letter to Charlie. In code!"

Ivan grinned back. They started writing. "Let's see if Charlie can figure that out, partner," said Ivan.

Ivan (code breaker 1234) and Ursula (code breaker 567583) shook hands.

DE36 CH3681E,
WE J57T 7082ED THE
837T C37E OF THE 1.C.
DETECT12E 3GE4CY.
F6OM
1234 & 567583
THE 1.C.5.
DETECT12E 3GE4CY

Think and Respond

How do Ivan's feelings change from the beginning to the end of the story?

Making Connections

Compare Texts

1 How does Beany grow and change in the story "The Talent Show"?

2 Who is the speaker or narrator in "The Talent Show"? How do you know?

3 Compare Beany from "The Talent Show" to Ivan from "The Last Case." How do Beany's and Ivan's feelings change?

4 "The Last Case of the I.C. Detective Agency" is a mystery. Think of another mystery story you have read or seen on television. Which mystery seemed more realistic? Explain why.

5 Do you think Beany and Carol Ann will continue to be friends after the talent show? Why or why not?

Write a Journal Entry

An important event in "The Talent Show" is Beany's talk with her dad. Write a journal entry that Beany might have written about that evening. Remember to use the pronouns *I, me,* and *we*. Answer these questions to gather ideas.

1. When and where did the talk take place?
2. What happened?
3. How did you feel?
4. What decision did you make?

Writing CONNECTION

Make a Poster

Beany and her dad could have used powerful telescopes to look at the stars. Do research to find information about one of the telescopes listed here. Create a poster. Name the telescope, tell where it is located, and add one or more interesting facts about it.

| Name of Telescope |
| Hale Telescope |
| Keck Telescope |
| Hubble Telescope |

Make an Estimate

There are too many stars for Beany to count, but scientists can estimate how many there are. You, too, can do an estimating activity.

Find an empty jar and some dried beans. Then estimate how many beans it will take to fill the jar. Write down your estimate. Here are some ideas to help you estimate.

- Cover the bottom of the jar with beans. Measure how high they are. Estimate how many layers it will take to fill the jar. Multiply the number of beans in the single layer by the number of layers.
- Count the number of beans it takes to fill the jar about a quarter of the way full. Multiply that number by four.

Prefixes and Suffixes

Look at the underlined words in these sentences.

Wendy is shy and talks quietly.

I don't think I've ever seen it so beautiful.

Beany's father sees that Beany is unhappy.

Each underlined word contains a prefix or a suffix.

- A **prefix** is a word part added to the **beginning** of a root word. It changes the word's meaning.

- A **suffix** is a word part added to the **end** of a root word. It changes the word's meaning.

If you know the meanings of prefixes and suffixes, you can figure out the meanings of many new words.

Root Word with Prefix or Suffix	Meaning of Prefix or Suffix	Meaning of New Word
bicycle	"two"	two-wheeled bike
impolite	"not"	not polite
happiness	"state of"	the state of being happy

Test Prep
Prefixes and Suffixes

> Josh and Tony had been playing ball <u>nonstop</u> for at least half an hour. Josh pitched, Tony hit, and Josh ran to get the ball. Then Josh pitched again, Tony hit, and Josh ran to get the ball. The same thing happened over and over. Josh was losing interest in playing ball with Tony.
>
> "Hey, Tony," he called in a <u>hopeful</u> voice, "how about letting me have a turn at bat?"

▶ Choose the group of words that best completes each sentence.

1. Adding the prefix <u>non</u> to <u>stop</u> changes the meaning to—

   A stopped again

   B with many stops

   C without stops

   D before a stop

Tip

Put the meaning of the prefix together with the root word to figure out the meaning of the new word.

2. The suffix <u>ful</u> in <u>hopeful</u> changes the meaning of <u>hope</u> to—

   F full of hope

   G without hope

   H having some hope

   J able to hope

Tip

Think of other words you know with this suffix, such as *helpful* or *colorful*.

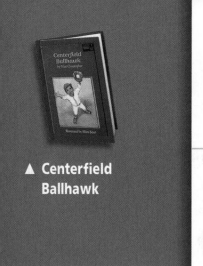

▲ Centerfield Ballhawk

vanish

outfielder

ballhawk

concentrate

depend

fault

Vocabulary Power

"**C**enterfield Ballhawk" is about a boy named José who wants his father to be proud of him. People are usually happy when they get along well with family members. Look at how this family gets along.

LANCE: Wow! Great catch! The game is over!

KAYLA: I thought that ball would **vanish**. It looked as if it would disappear over the fence.

LANCE: If I were a baseball player, I'd want to be an **outfielder**. When you play in the outfield, it's up to you to catch the fly balls that go far back in the field.

KAYLA: To be a great outfielder, you have to be a **ballhawk**. A ballhawk always seems to be able to catch the ball wherever it goes.

MOTHER: OK, you two, the game is over. Now it's time to **concentrate** on your homework. You need to pay close attention to that project you're working on, Lance.

LANCE: Oh, Mom, you know you can **depend** on me to get it done.

MOTHER: Yes, I can always trust you to do your work on time, Lance.

KAYLA: Remember the time I forgot to do my math? It was mostly my **fault**, but Lance was a little bit to blame, too. He had me so busy helping him with his joke book that I forgot my own work!

Vocabulary–Writing CONNECTION

Write a paragraph that describes what can happen to an **outfielder** or another ball player who fails to **concentrate** on the game.

Centerfield
Ballhawk
by Matt Christopher

Award-Winning
Author

Realistic Fiction

Realistic fiction tells about characters and events that are like people and events in real life.

In this selection, look for

- **problems that could happen in real life.**

- **special words that tell about baseball.**

CENTERFIELD BALLHAWK

by Matt Christopher
illustrated by Larry Johnson

José Mendez knew better than to play baseball in the front yard. While practicing his batting, he hit a ball through Mrs. Dooley's car window! Now Mr. Mendez is really disappointed in José. José thinks there's only one way to make his father proud of him again.

José's father once played in the minor leagues. José's sister, Carmen, plays softball and has been hitting balls over the fence. José thinks that if he becomes a better batter, everything will be all right once more.

"Steeerike!" yelled the ump. Then, "Steeerike two!"

"Belt it, José!" cried the coach.

José's heart pounded like crazy. This was it.

Crack! His bat met the ball head-on. The white sphere took off like a rocket for left field and sailed over the fence for a home run!

The Mudders' fans screamed their heads off. "All right, José!" they shouted as he dropped his bat and trotted around the bases.

Bus singled that inning, too, but the Mudders failed to score him. Mudders 5, Bulls 2.

The Stockade Bulls came to bat blowing through their nostrils. After two outs and a man on third base, Adzie Healy lambasted one. It had a home run label on it as it zoomed toward the center field fence. José started to run back the instant he had seen it hit.

He was almost up against the fence when the ball came flying down over his head. He jumped—and caught it!

"Yes! Great catch, man!" Barry yelled. "Saved us a run!"

José smiled and tossed the ball to him as they ran in together. "Just lucky," he said.

"Sure." Barry laughed.

Alfie singled, and Turtleneck walked, bringing José up to the plate. *I've got to get a hit*, he thought. *I've got to, or I'm sunk.*

He grounded out.

Good thing Dad isn't at the game, he thought as he returned to the bench. At least he's got Carmen.

The Mudders kept the Bulls from scoring in the bottom of the fourth and then went to town at their turn at bat, scoring two runs. Mudders 7, Bulls 2.

In the bottom of the fifth, the Stockade Bulls showed the real power they had, as if they had purposely kept it hidden until now. They pounded Sparrow for five runs, tying up the score, 7 to 7.

In the top of the sixth, Barry singled, then Turtleneck flied out. José slowly stepped to the plate. This could be it, he thought. A hit now could break the tie. And it would mean a .500 average for him.

He flied out.

José's heart sank into his stomach. He wished he could vanish.

Then T.V. struck out, and the Bulls were back up to the plate.

The first two guys got on. Then Ted Jackson popped up to the pitcher, and Adzie blasted a line drive to center field. It looked as if it were going to hit the ground halfway between second base and José.

José was after it like a gazelle. He knew he had to catch that ball or the game was over.

He dove, then felt the solid *thud!* as the ball landed squarely in his glove.

The crowd stood up, and clapped and cheered for a full minute.

On the next play, a grounder skittered through T.V.'s legs. A run scored, and the game was over. The Stockade Bulls beat the Peach Street Mudders, 8 to 7.

"It's my fault we lost! My fault!" T.V. moaned as José caught up with him and they walked off the field together.

"Don't sweat it, man!" José said. "It's not the end of the world! Who's perfect?"

He was thinking of his batting as he said it. One out of four was .250. Far, far from a .375 average. His father would never, *never* think much of him as a baseball player.

Suddenly he heard his name called. "José! Wait up!"

He turned.

"Dad!" he cried, surprised. "When did you get here?"

"At the beginning of the fourth inning," Mr. Mendez said.

José's face clouded. "Then you saw . . ." he started to say, but couldn't go on. How could he face his father when he'd gotten out three out of four times at bat?

"What do you want to say, son?" Mr. Mendez asked, putting his arm across José's shoulders.

"I wanted to make you proud of me," José blurted out. "I know I've been messing up lately, but I thought if I could hit .375, like you did when you played in the minors, I could make up for disappointing you. I—I'm sorry, Dad. I know I've let you down."

Mr. Mendez stopped short and looked down at José. "Is that why you've been so down in the mouth?" he exclaimed.

José sighed, then nodded.

"Listen, son," Mr. Mendez said, "I may be disappointed when you go against my wishes—like you did when you hit Mrs. Dooley's car—but I'm not disappointed in *you*. I trust you when you say you're sorry, and that's that. As far as Mrs. Dooley is concerned, I know you've worked hard to make it up to her. From what I hear," he added, smiling, "you even applied a little extra elbow grease to her car the other day."

José blushed.

Then Mr. Mendez took a deep breath and went on: "It's been hard since Mom died . . . on all of us. I've had to depend on you and Carmen to pull your own weight . . . maybe too much." He grinned. "I seem to have forgotten how hard it can be to concentrate on anything when it's baseball season. Maybe we both need to be more aware of what the other person is feeling. I'll try, if you will."

José nodded happily.

"And one more thing. Forget about trying to hit like I did, okay? You don't have to. You're a born outfielder, José! You've made catches that I never would have been able to, not in a million years."

José stared at him. "Really? You mean you . . . don't mind that I can't hit?"

José's father chuckled. "'Can't hit?' If you call belting a grand slam homer not hitting, well, son, we've got to sit down and have a serious talk about the game of baseball! José, you're a born ballhawk, so stop worrying about the hitting and concentrate on your fielding. That's where your team needs you the most."

José couldn't believe his ears. All this time he had thought . . . But then he recalled the joyous cheers after each catch he had made that day and smiled.

"Thanks, Dad," he murmured. "I never thought about that. I just figured the guys were being nice when they said they counted on me being in the outfield." He glanced up at his father. "I like having people depend on me, Dad."

His father squeezed his shoulder. "Come on. We'll pick up some ice cream and celebrate those catches with Carmen. I understand she's had a hard afternoon, smashing one homer after another for her team. Looks like both of you kids are a chip off the old block, eh?"

José laughed. He never felt better in his life as he walked with his father to the car.

I might never get a .375 average, he thought. But I'm a hit with my father, and that's what counts the most.

THINK AND RESPOND

1. What does José learn about his father and about himself?

2. The author uses **ballhawk** and **outfielder** to describe José. How are these words alike or different?

3. How can you tell that José is unhappy when he finds out his father has watched the game?

4. If you played baseball, would you want to be on the same team as José? Why or why not?

5. Explain how using a reading strategy helped you in reading this selection.

About the Author

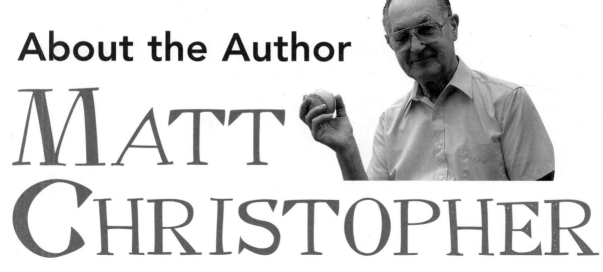

MATT CHRISTOPHER

As a boy, Matt Christopher had two favorite hobbies: sports and writing. He played all kinds of sports, but he liked baseball the best. When he first started playing baseball, he sometimes got discouraged because he wasn't a star batter. When he got older, he played so well that he earned a Most Valuable Player award.

Later, instead of playing sports, Matt Christopher began writing about them. During his life, he wrote more than seventy-five books. He once said, "I love writing and do as most writers do: work on an idea until it's the best I can come up with. Then I work on another... and another... and so on!"

Visit *The Learning Site!*
www.harcourtschool.com

SPOTLIGHT ON BASEBALL

Baseball is a popular game in many parts of the world. The diagram below shows how a baseball field is set up. The text on page 351 gives more information about the centerfielder.

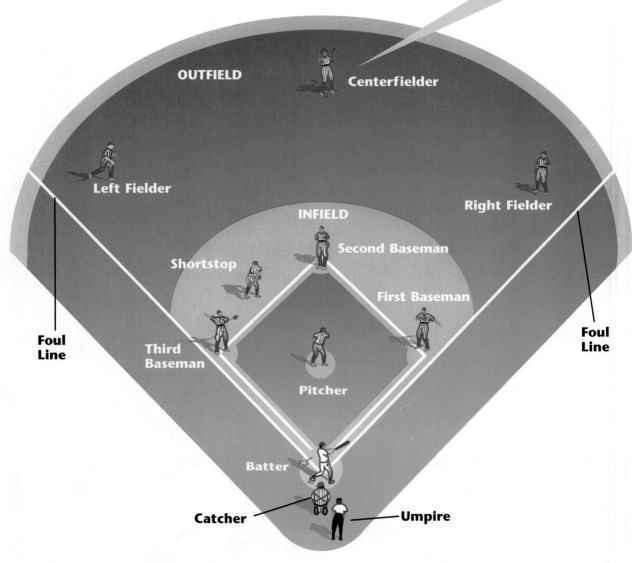

OUTFIELD

Centerfielder

Left Fielder

Right Fielder

INFIELD

Second Baseman

Shortstop

First Baseman

Foul Line

Third Baseman

Foul Line

Pitcher

Batter

Catcher

Umpire

José Mendez plays center field for his baseball team, the Peach Street Mudders. Center field is one of the most important positions in baseball. Read below to find out more about what a centerfielder does.

Centerfielder

The centerfielder should be the best all-around outfielder on the team. The centerfielder is considered the captain of the outfield. He or she should be the outfielder with the most speed. This is because the centerfielder has the most ground to cover. The centerfielder must also have a very strong arm. He or she has to make long throws and move like a cat. The centerfielder must be able to quickly run in, run back, or run to either side.

The centerfielder should try to catch any fly balls he or she can reach. The other outfielders run for fly balls until they hear the centerfielder "call them off."

Center field is fun. It is also a very important position. Some of the best players in history have played center field.

THINK AND RESPOND

Why is center field an important position in baseball?

Making Connections

Compare Texts

1. Why does "Centerfield Ballhawk" belong in a theme about changing and growing?

2. Compare José's reaction to T.V.'s performance in the game with his reaction to his own performance.

3. Do you think José's father would agree with the author's point of view in "Spotlight on Baseball"? Why or why not?

4. Look back to the selection "A Guide to Basketball," on page 122. How are the two articles alike and different?

5. Do you think José will keep trying to improve his batting? Explain your answer.

Write a Sportscast

Sportscasters on the radio describe games so that listeners can picture what is happening. Choose one inning in the game between the Mudders and the Bulls. Write one paragraph that a sportscaster might use to tell what is happening. Make your sportscast exciting for listeners. Use a graphic organizer like the one shown here to organize your thoughts.

Writing
CONNECTION

Sequence of events in the game

First, _____

Then, _____

Next, _____

Create a Baseball Quiz

José shared a love of baseball with his friends and his family. Use the Internet or print sources to find out about important events in the history of baseball. On one side of a sheet of paper, write quiz questions about four or five important events or players. List the answers on the back. Add illustrations or a border to make your quiz look inviting. Exchange quizzes with classmates, and see how many questions you can answer.

Chart of the Best Pitchers

José's father in "Centerfield Ballhawk" was a great hitter. Pitchers try to strike out hitters. During a baseball career, some pitchers have managed to strike out thousands of hitters. Use reference sources to find the five pitchers who have had the most strikeouts. Make a chart to show their records. You might add a column to show what team each played for.

Pitcher	Career Strikeouts
Nolan Ryan	(number)
(name)	(number)

Sequence

Authors use time-order clues to help readers understand the sequence of events.

After two outs and with a player on third base, Adzie Healy lambasted one.

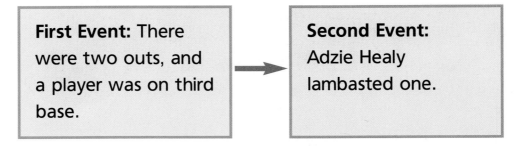

| **First Event:** There were two outs, and a player was on third base. | → | **Second Event:** Adzie Healy lambasted one. |

José smiled and tossed the ball to Adzie as they ran in together.

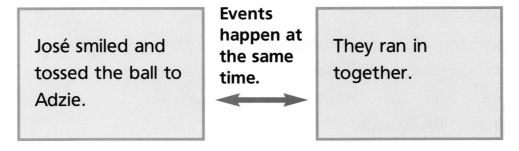

| José smiled and tossed the ball to Adzie. | **Events happen at the same time.** ←→ | They ran in together. |

Dates are also time-order clues that tell about sequence.

The game took place on Tuesday, April 16.

José's father hit three home runs on July 8, 1988.

Test Prep
Sequence

▶ **Read the story. Then answer numbers 1 and 2.**

> The Eagles played the Panthers on June 5. After the first eight innings, neither team had scored. Then, with two outs in the last inning, Kayla hit a home run! The Eagles won.
>
> Two weeks later, on June 19, the two teams played again. The game was almost over, and the Eagles were losing. If Kayla could hit a home run, her team would win. Kayla swung and missed twice. Finally, she swung with all her might. "Strike three!" called the umpire. The Eagles lost the game, but Kayla and her teammates did not lose hope. "We'll win next time!" they said.

1. **Which event happened first?**

    A The teams played again on June 19.

    B Carmen got on base.

    C Kayla hit a home run.

    D Kayla swung and missed.

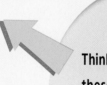

Tip

Think about which of these events happened first in the story.

2. **What happened after Kayla hit a home run?**

    F The Eagles won the game.

    G There were two outs in the last inning.

    H The Eagles were losing.

    J The Eagles and Panthers played on June 5.

Tip

Find in the story where Kayla hit a home run. Which choice comes next in the story?

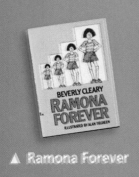

▲ Ramona Forever

Vocabulary Power

- contagious
- prescription
- comfort
- longed
- glanced
- attention
- unexpected

There are many ways to show kindness to family members and friends. Here are some things Steven did to make his friend Brianna feel better when she was sick.

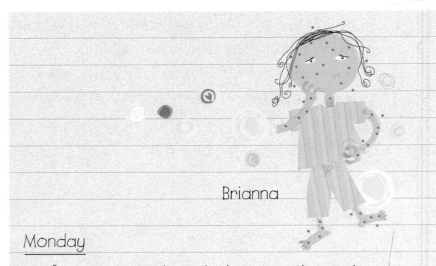

Brianna

Monday

My friend Brianna has chicken pox. She can't come to school because chicken pox is **contagious**. That means people can catch it by being close to someone who has it. I hope she gets better soon.

Wednesday

I called Brianna yesterday. She was itchy, but the doctor wrote a **prescription** for medicine to help her with that. It gave her some **comfort**, and she felt better. What she wanted most was to see her friends. She **longed** to have someone to talk to and play games with.

Thursday

Today I had a great idea. After school, I took some paper and markers to Brianna's house and tapped on her window. She looked sad when she first **glanced** out, but after that quick look she smiled and waved.

We wrote notes to each other and held them up to the window. Then we played tic-tac-toe. I think Brianna was happy with the **attention** I gave her. Showing kindness makes people feel good. Before I went home, Brianna held up a note.

Thanks, Steven! Your **unexpected** visit was a nice surprise. I feel a lot better!

Vocabulary–Writing CONNECTION

Write five sentences. In each one, tell a way in which you can give a sick person **attention** and **comfort**.

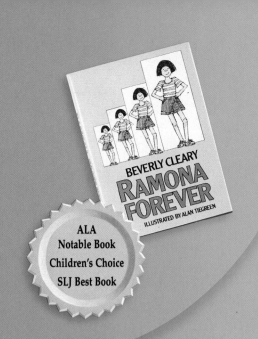

ALA
Notable Book
Children's Choice
SLJ Best Book

Genre

Realistic Fiction

Realistic fiction tells about characters and events that are like people and events in real life.

In this selection, look for

- **one main character.**

- **a plot with a beginning, a middle, and an end.**

Ramona Forever

by Beverly Cleary

illustrated by Diane Greenseid

After Uncle Hobart's exciting wedding, the Quimby family is about to have another big event — the birth of the fifth Quimby. The baby, whom they have all nicknamed Algie, will be born today!

Mrs. Quimby pushed her chair farther from the table and glanced at her watch. All eyes were on her.

"Shall I call the doctor?" asked Mr. Quimby.

"Please," said Mrs. Quimby as she rose from the table, hugged Algie, and breathed, "Oo-oo."

Ramona and Beezus, excited and frightened, looked at one another. At last! The fifth Quimby would soon be here. Nothing would be the same again, ever. Mr. Quimby reported that the doctor would meet them at the hospital. Without being asked, Beezus ran for the bag her mother had packed several weeks ago.

Mrs. Quimby kissed her daughters. "Don't look so frightened," she said. "Everything is going to be all right. Be good girls, and Daddy will be home as soon as he can." She bent forward and hugged Algie again.

The house suddenly seemed empty. The girls listened to the car back out of the driveway. The sound of the motor became lost in traffic.

"Well," said Beezus, "I suppose we might as well do the dishes."

"I suppose so." Ramona tested all the doors, including the door to the basement, to make sure they were locked.

"Too bad Picky-picky isn't here to eat all this tuna salad no one felt like eating." Beezus scraped the plates into the garbage.

To her own surprise, Ramona burst into tears and buried her face in a dish towel. "I just want Mother to come home," she wept.

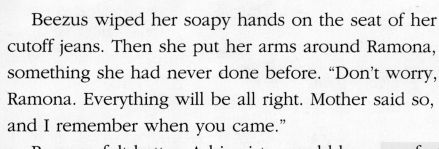

Beezus wiped her soapy hands on the seat of her cutoff jeans. Then she put her arms around Ramona, something she had never done before. "Don't worry, Ramona. Everything will be all right. Mother said so, and I remember when you came."

Ramona felt better. A big sister could be a comfort if she wanted to.

"You got born and Mother was fine." Beezus handed Ramona a clean dish towel.

Minutes crawled by. The long Oregon dusk turned into night. The girls turned on the television set to a program about people in a hospital, running, shouting, giving orders. Quickly they turned it off. "I hope Aunt Bea and Uncle Hobart are all right," said Ramona. The girls longed for their loving aunt, who was cheerful in times of trouble and who was always there when the family needed her. Now she was in a truck, riding along the Canadian Highway to Alaska. Ramona thought about bears, mean bears. She wondered if two pairs of white shoes still danced from the bumper of the truck.

The ring of the telephone made Ramona feel as if arrows of electricity had shot through her stomach as Beezus ran to answer.

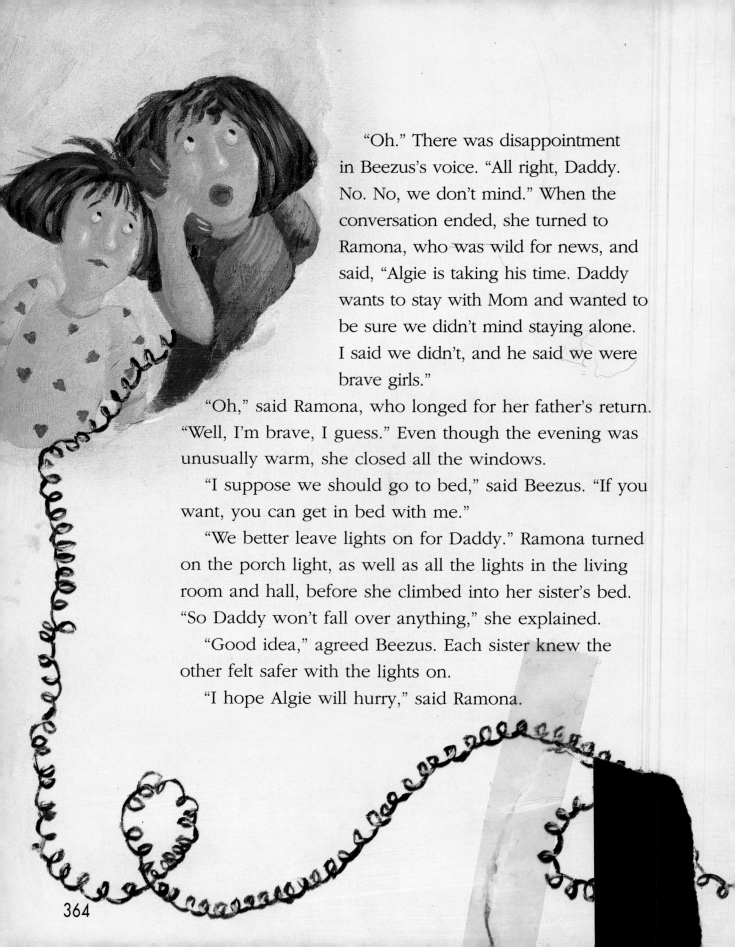

"Oh." There was disappointment in Beezus's voice. "All right, Daddy. No. No, we don't mind." When the conversation ended, she turned to Ramona, who was wild for news, and said, "Algie is taking his time. Daddy wants to stay with Mom and wanted to be sure we didn't mind staying alone. I said we didn't, and he said we were brave girls."

"Oh," said Ramona, who longed for her father's return. "Well, I'm brave, I guess." Even though the evening was unusually warm, she closed all the windows.

"I suppose we should go to bed," said Beezus. "If you want, you can get in bed with me."

"We better leave lights on for Daddy." Ramona turned on the porch light, as well as all the lights in the living room and hall, before she climbed into her sister's bed. "So Daddy won't fall over anything," she explained.

"Good idea," agreed Beezus. Each sister knew the other felt safer with the lights on.

"I hope Algie will hurry," said Ramona.

"So do I," agreed Beezus.

The girls slept lightly until the sound of a key in the door awoke them. "Daddy?" Beezus called out.

"Yes." Mr. Quimby came down the hall to the door of Beezus's room. "Great news. Roberta Day Quimby, six pounds, four ounces, arrived safe and sound. Your mother is fine."

Barely awake, Ramona asked, "Who's Roberta?"

"Your new sister," answered her father, "and my namesake."

"*Sister.*" Now Ramona was wide-awake. The family had referred to the baby as Algie so long she had assumed that of course she would have a brother.

"Yes, a beautiful little sister," said her father. "Now, go back to sleep. It's four o'clock in the morning, and I've got to get up at seven-thirty."

The next morning, Mr. Quimby overslept and ate his breakfast standing up. He was halfway out the door when he called back, "When I get off work, we'll have dinner at the Whopperburger, and then we'll all go see Roberta and your mother."

The day was long and lonely. Even a swimming lesson at the park and a trip to the library did little to make time pass. "I wonder what Roberta looks like?" said Beezus.

"And whose room she will share when she outgrows the bassinette?" worried Ramona.

The one happy moment in the day for the girls was a telephone call from their mother, who reported that Roberta was a beautiful, healthy little sister. She couldn't wait to bring her home, and she was proud of her daughters for being so good about staying alone. This pleased Beezus and Ramona so much they ran the vacuum cleaner and dusted, which made time pass faster until their father, looking exhausted, came home to take them out for hamburgers and a visit to the fifth Quimby.

Ramona could feel her heart pounding as she finally climbed the steps to the hospital. Visitors, some carrying flowers and others looking careworn, walked toward the elevators. Nurses hurried, a doctor was paged over the loudspeaker. Ramona could scarcely bear her own excitement. The rising of the elevator made her stomach feel as if it had stayed behind on the first floor. When the elevator stopped, Mr. Quimby led the way down the hall.

"Excuse me," called a nurse.

Surprised, the family stopped and turned.

"Children under twelve are not allowed to visit the maternity ward," said the nurse. "Little girl, you will have to go down and wait in the lobby."

"Why is that?" asked Mr. Quimby.

"Children under twelve might have contagious diseases," explained the nurse. "We have to protect the babies."

"I'm sorry, Ramona," said Mr. Quimby. "I didn't know. I am afraid you will have to do as the nurse says."

"Does she mean I'm *germy*?" Ramona was humiliated. "I took a shower this morning and washed my hands at the Whopperburger so I would be extra clean."

"Sometimes children are coming down with something and don't know it," explained Mr. Quimby. "Now, be a big girl and go downstairs and wait for us."

Ramona's eyes filled with tears of disappointment, but she found some pleasure in riding in the elevator alone. By the time she reached the lobby, she felt worse. The nurse called her a little girl. Her father called her a big girl. What was she? A germy girl.

Ramona sat gingerly on the edge of a Naugahyde couch. If she leaned back, she might get germs on it, or it might get germs on her. She swallowed hard. Was her throat a little bit sore? She thought maybe it was, way down in back. She put her hand to her forehead the way her mother did when she thought Ramona might have a fever. Her forehead was warm, maybe too warm.

As Ramona waited, she began to itch the way she itched when she had chickenpox. Her head itched, her back itched, her legs itched. Ramona scratched. A woman sat down on the couch, looked at Ramona, got up, and moved to another couch.

Ramona felt worse. She itched more and scratched harder. She swallowed often to see how her sore throat was coming along. She peeked down the neck of her blouse to see if she might have a rash and was surprised that she did not. She sniffed from time to time to see if she had a runny nose.

Now Ramona was angry. It would serve everybody right if she came down with some horrible disease, right there in their old hospital. That would show everybody how germfree the place was. Ramona squirmed and gave that hard-to-reach place between her shoulder blades a good hard scratch. Then she scratched her head with both hands. People stopped to stare.

A man in a white coat, with a stethoscope hanging out of his pocket, came hurrying through the lobby, glanced at Ramona, stopped, and took a good look at her. "How do you feel?" he asked.

"Awful," she admitted. "A nurse said I was too germy to go see my mother and new sister, but I think I caught some disease right here."

"I see," said the doctor. "Open your mouth and say 'ah.'"

Ramona *ahhed* until she gagged.

"Mh-hm," murmured the doctor. He looked so serious Ramona was alarmed. Then he pulled out his stethoscope and listened to her front and back, thumping as he did so. What was he hearing? Was there something wrong with her insides? Why didn't her father come?

The doctor nodded as if his worst suspicions had been confirmed. "Just as I thought," he said, pulling out his prescription pad.

Medicine, ugh. Ramona's twitching stopped. Her nose and throat felt fine. "I feel much better," she assured the doctor as she eyed that prescription pad with distrust.

"An acute case of siblingitis. Not at all unusual around here, but it shouldn't last long." He tore off the prescription he had written, instructed Ramona to give it to her father, and hurried on down the hall.

Ramona could not remember the name of her illness. She tried to read the doctor's scribbly cursive writing, but she could not. She could only read neat cursive, the sort her teacher wrote on the blackboard.

Itching again, she was still staring at the slip of paper when Mr. Quimby and Beezus stepped out of the elevator. "Roberta is so tiny." Beezus was radiant with joy. "And she is perfectly darling. She has a little round nose and—oh, when you see her, you'll love her."

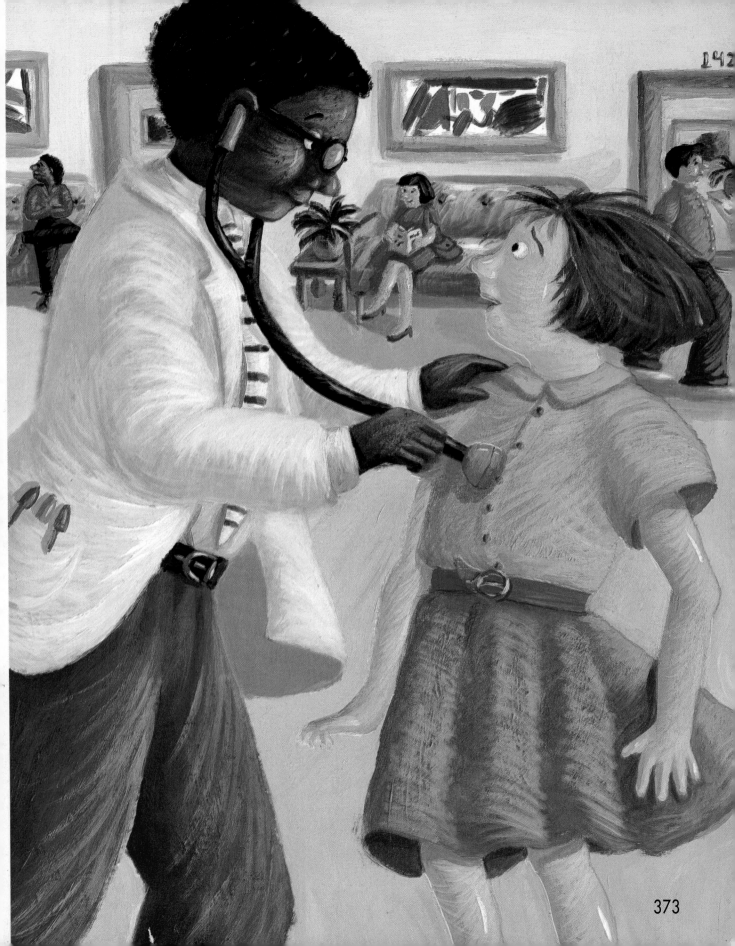

"I'm sick." Ramona tried to sound pitiful. "I've got something awful. A doctor said so."

Beezus paid no attention. "And Roberta has brown hair —"

Mr. Quimby interrupted. "What's this all about, Ramona?"

"A doctor said I had something, some kind of *itis*, and I have to have this right away." She handed her father her prescription and scratched one shoulder. "If I don't, I might get sicker."

Mr. Quimby read the scribbly cursive, and then he did a strange thing. He lifted Ramona and gave her a big hug and a kiss, right there in the lobby. The itching stopped. Ramona felt much better. "You have acute siblingitis," explained her father. *"Itis* means inflammation."

Ramona already knew the meaning of sibling. Since her father had studied to be a teacher, brothers and sisters had become siblings to him.

"He understood you were worried and angry because you weren't allowed to see your new sibling, and prescribed attention," explained Mr. Quimby. "Now let's all go buy ice-cream cones before I fall asleep standing up."

Beezus said Roberta was too darling to be called a dumb word like sibling. Ramona felt silly, but she also felt better.

For the next three nights, Ramona took a book to the hospital and sat in the lobby, not reading, but sulking about the injustice of having to wait to see the strange new Roberta.

On the fourth day, Mr. Quimby took an hour off from the Shop-rite Market, picked up Beezus and Ramona, who were waiting in clean clothes, and drove to the hospital to bring home his wife and new daughter.

Ramona moved closer to Beezus when she saw her mother, holding a pink bundle, emerge from the elevator in a wheelchair pushed by a nurse and followed by Mr. Quimby carrying her bag. "Can't Mother walk?" she whispered.

"Of course she can walk," answered Beezus. "The hospital wants to make sure people get out without falling down and suing for a million dollars."

Mrs. Quimby waved to the girls. Roberta's face was hidden by a corner of a pink blanket, but the nurse had no time for a little girl eager to see a new baby. She pushed the wheelchair through the automatic door to the waiting car.

"*Now* can I see her?" begged Ramona when her mother and Roberta were settled in the front, and the girls had climbed into the backseat.

"Dear Heart, of course you may." Mrs. Quimby then spoke the most beautiful words Ramona had ever heard, "Oh, Ramona, how I've missed you," as she turned back the blanket.

Ramona, leaning over the front seat for her first

glimpse of the new baby sister, tried to hold her breath so she wouldn't breathe germs on Roberta, who did not look at all like the picture on the cover of *A Name for Your Baby*. Her face was bright pink, almost red, and her hair, unlike the smooth pale hair of the baby on the cover of the pamphlet, was dark and wild. Ramona did not know what to say. She did not feel that words like darling or adorable fitted this baby.

"She looks exactly like you looked when you were born," Mrs. Quimby told Ramona.

"She does?" Ramona found this hard to believe. She could not imagine that she had once looked like this red, frowning little creature.

"Well, what do you think of your new sister?" asked Mr. Quimby.

"She's so—so *little*," Ramona answered truthfully.

Roberta opened her blue gray eyes.

"Mother!" cried Ramona. "She's cross-eyed."

Mrs. Quimby laughed. "All babies look cross-eyed sometimes. They outgrow it when they learn to focus." Sure enough, Roberta's eyes straightened out for a moment and then crossed again. She worked her mouth as if she didn't know what to do with it. She made little snuffling noises and lifted one arm as if she didn't know what it was for.

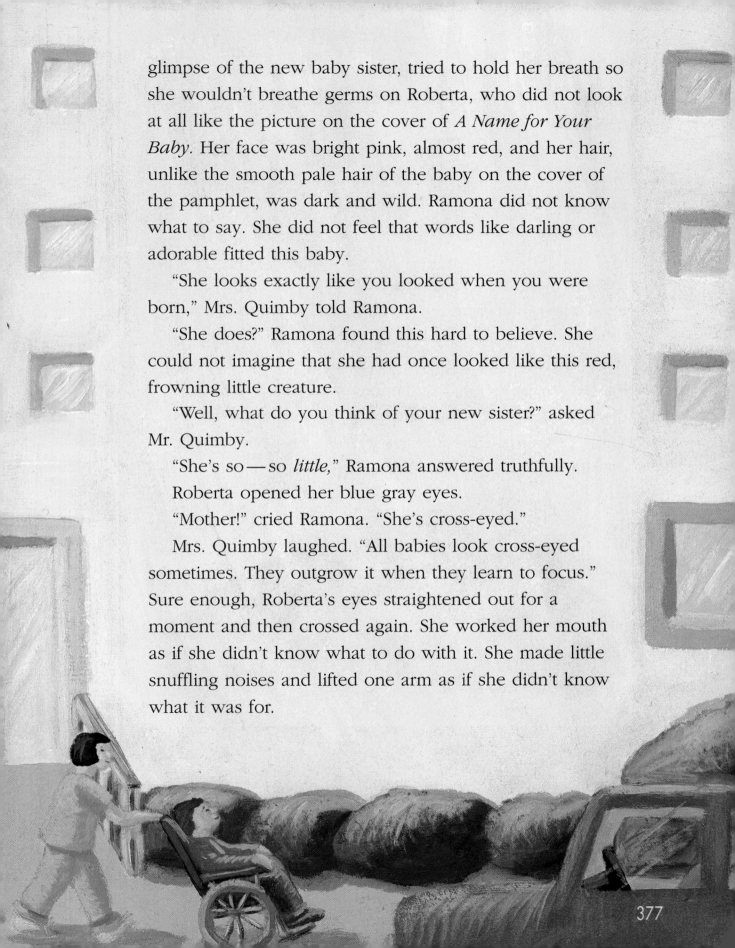

"Why does her nightie have those little pockets at the ends of the sleeves?" asked Ramona. "They cover up her hands."

"They keep her from scratching herself," explained Mrs. Quimby. "She's too little to understand that fingernails scratch."

Ramona sat back and buckled her seat belt. She had once looked like Roberta. Amazing! She had once been that tiny, but she had grown, her hair had calmed down when she remembered to comb it, and she had learned to use her eyes and hands. "You know what I think?" she asked and did not wait for an answer. "I think it is hard work to be a baby." Ramona spoke as if she had discovered something unknown to the rest of the world. With her words came unexpected love and sympathy for the tiny person in her mother's arms.

"I hadn't thought of it that way," said Mrs. Quimby, "but I think you're right."

"Growing up is hard work," said Mr. Quimby as he drove away from the hospital. "Sometimes being grown-up is hard work."

"I know," said Ramona and thought some more. She thought about loose teeth, real sore throats, quarrels, misunderstandings with her teachers, longing for a bicycle her family could not afford, worrying when her parents bickered, how terrible she had felt when she hurt Beezus's feelings without meaning to, and all the long afternoons when Mrs. Kemp looked after her until her mother came from work. She had survived it all. "Isn't it funny?" she remarked as her father steered the car into their driveway.

"Isn't what funny?" asked her mother.

"That I used to be little and funny-looking and cross-eyed like Roberta," said Ramona. "And now look at me. I'm wonderful me!"

"Except when you're blunderful you," said Beezus.

Ramona did not mind when her family, except Roberta, who was too little, laughed. "Yup, wonderful, blunderful me," she said and was happy. She was winning at growing up.

Think and Respond

1. What is Ramona's problem? How do her parents help her?

2. Why does Ramona think she is "winning at growing up"?

3. What is "siblingitis"? Explain it in your own words.

4. Do you think the doctor wrote a good **prescription?** Why or why not?

5. Give an example of a reading strategy that you used while reading this selection.

Meet the Author
Beverly Cleary

How does Beverly Cleary write? Read this interview to find out.

Question: How do you actually do your writing?

Beverly Cleary: Oh, I write with a pen first. Then I type up what I've written so I can see what it looks like.

Question: What is the hardest thing for you about writing, and what is the easiest thing?

Beverly Cleary: The hardest thing about writing is pushing through to the end of the story. The easiest thing is revising. I think all writers do some revising. That is when I cross out a lot and shorten a page to one paragraph.

Question: When you start a book, do you know how it's going to end?

Beverly Cleary: I often begin in the middle. I begin with the characters and something they would do and just let the story work itself out.

ALL MY HATS

by Richard J. Margolis
illustrated by Robert Casilla

All my hats
are hats he wore.
What a bore.

All my pants
are pants he ripped.
What a gyp.

All my books
are books he read.
What a head.

All my fights
are fights he fought.
What a thought.

All my steps
are steps he tried.
What a guide.

All my teachers
call me by my brother's name.
What a shame.

Making Connections

Compare Texts

1 What important change takes place in Ramona's life? What does she learn from this experience?

2 Why does the illustrator show three different pictures on page 370 of Ramona on the couch?

3 The younger brother in the poem "All My Hats" seems to have a case of "siblingitis." If Ramona could give him some advice, what do you think she would tell him?

4 Compare the characters and events in "Ramona Forever" with another realistic fiction story you've read.

5 Do you think Ramona will enjoy being Roberta's big sister? Why or why not?

Write a Paragraph

Growing up is hard work, but Ramona is doing quite well. Write a paragraph about a time that you learned something important about growing up. You can jot down a list of ideas for your paragraph.

Lessons I've Learned

1.

2.

3.

Writing CONNECTION

Create a Display

In "Ramona Forever," the doctor listens to Ramona's heart with a stethoscope. Do research to find information about your heart. What does it look like? Why is it so important? What does the doctor hear when he or she listens to your heart? Create a display to share the information you find. You might draw pictures or diagrams, or write a research paper about the heart.

Research Birth Rate

Like Ramona's sister, babies are born every day. Find out about the number of births in your area and in four other areas of the United States in a given year. Why are certain areas of the country more populated than others? Show your findings on a copy of a United States map.

Prefixes and Suffixes

Look at the underlined word in each sentence. How does adding a prefix or suffix change the meaning of the word?

Beezus thinks Roberta is <u>adorable</u>.

adore + able = adorable (can be adored)

"I feel much better," she assured the doctor as she eyed the prescription pad with <u>distrust</u>.

dis + trust = distrust (the opposite of *trust*)

Ramona sulked about the <u>injustice</u> of having to wait to see the strange new Roberta.

in + justice = injustice (no justice; unfair)

The suffix *ful* means "full of." What does *wonderful* mean? What do you think the made-up word *blunderful* means?

**Visit *The Learning Site!*
www.harcourtschool.com**

See *Skills* and *Activities*

Test Prep
Prefixes and Suffixes

> It seemed <u>impossible</u> to Ricardo that his tiny new baby brother would ever be big enough to play with him. Ricardo treated little Roberto very <u>carefully</u>. For now, Roberto was <u>helpless</u>. All he could do was eat, sleep, and cry.

1. The word <u>impossible</u> means—

   A possible again

   B more possible

   C almost possible

   D not possible

Tip
Put the meaning of the prefix together with the root word.

2. The word <u>carefully</u> means—

   F in a way that is full of care

   G able to be cared for

   H in a way that cares again

   J without care

Tip
Use the definition of both suffixes to determine meaning.

3. The word <u>helpless</u> means—

   A able to help again

   B not able to help himself

   C not in need of help

   D helped earlier

Tip
Think of other words you know with this suffix, such as *useless* or *restless*.

▲ Sayings We Share

Vocabulary Power

In the selection "Sayings We Share," you will read some wise sayings. These sayings have been passed down over many years. We can learn a great deal from the lessons of the past.

generation

summoned

faithful

persistently

illuminated

fortunate

Town Heroes Honored

The base of this new flagpole honors heroes of the past.

Our town has a new base for its flagpole. On it are words that honor the people of our grandparents' **generation**, or age group, who saved the town from a flood many years ago. It had rained for days, and the river began to overflow. Citizens were **summoned** to help build a wall of sandbags that would hold back the water. Everyone who was sent for came out willingly.

Stopping the flood was an enormous job, but the people were **faithful** in their promise to get it done. They worked **persistently**, all through the night, never stopping or giving up as the river rose higher and higher. Only the light from their lanterns and flashlights **illuminated** the place where they worked. At last the rain stopped. The wall had saved the town!

We are **fortunate** that these brave people built that wall. We feel lucky and are proud to remember what they did.

Vocabulary–Writing
CONNECTION

Write a paragraph about a job or a skill you had to work at or practice **persistently**.

Sayings We Share

Proverbs and Fables

compiled by *Norma Tong Lee*
illustrated by *Krystyna Stasiak*

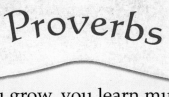

Proverbs

As you grow, you learn much about life from the people around you. Older family members often teach you what the world is like and how to be a good person. One way that people teach each other about life is through *oral traditions*. These are stories and sayings that are passed down from generation to generation.

The *proverb* is one kind of oral tradition. Proverbs are common sayings. Different cultures and languages sometimes have very similar proverbs. Here are examples of proverbs that are similar in different languages:

In the United States, people say "Don't spread yourself too thin." In Vietnam, people say "Even with two hands, one cannot catch two fish at one time." Both proverbs mean that it is better to do one thing well than to do many things poorly. In some parts of Africa, people say "As a crab walks, so walk its children." In the United States, people say "Like father, like son." The words are different, but the ideas are the same.

Vietnamese Proverbs

Here are more Vietnamese proverbs, with similar sayings in English.

* Working persistently, ants can fill the nest with food.
  One beaver can fell a hundred trees.

* Silence is gold, words are silver.
  Silence is golden.

* Near the ink, one is stained black; near the lamp, one is illuminated.
  He who keeps company with wolves will learn to howl.

* If bamboo is not shaped when young, it will explode when old.
  You can't teach an old dog new tricks.

When hulling rice, one cannot carry one's baby sister.
One cannot be in two places at once.

Other Well-Known Proverbs

🌷 He who lies down with dogs, shall rise up with fleas.

🌷 One today is worth two tomorrows.

🌷 You may delay, but time will not.

🌷 A sleeping cat cannot catch a rat.

🌷 A wise man hears one word and understands two.

🌷 There are two sides to every story.

🌷 A penny saved is a penny earned.

🌷 Early to bed and early to rise makes a man healthy, wealthy, and wise.

🌷 Hunger never saw bad bread.

Fables

The *fable* is another type of oral tradition. A fable is a short tale that teaches something about life. Many fables use animal characters to act out a simple lesson. Like proverbs, fables are told in families and are often passed down from generation to generation. Some of the best-known fables are called Aesop's Fables. These were told more than 2000 years ago by a man named Aesop (ē′säp). The fables on the next pages come from different cultures all over the world. Each of these fables has a moral. A moral is like a proverb because it tells what the story should teach you. Do you recognize some of these fables?

by Aesop

The Hare and the Tortoise

"Tortoise, you're such a slowpoke," said Hare. "Me, I'm really fast."

Tortoise replied, "I get to where I'm going in my own good time." And she challenged Hare to a race.

"A race? Against *me*?" Hare laughed and laughed. "All right. I'll race you down to that willow tree. Ready, get set, go!"

He sprinted forward, lightning fast.

Tortoise set off at her pace.

In a jiffy Hare was more than half the way there. "I'll take a little nap," he thought, and stretched out in the sun.

He slept while Tortoise lumbered along.

On she lumbered, slow and steady . . .

When Hare awoke, Tortoise had nearly reached the willow.

Hare jumped up and ran and ran and ran . . . but too late. Tortoise won!

> MORAL *Slow and steady wins the race.*

by Arnold Lobel

The Young Rooster

A young Rooster was summoned to his Father's bedside.

"Son, my time has come to an end," said the aged bird. "Now it is your turn to crow up the morning sun each day."

The young Rooster watched sadly as his Father's life slipped away.

Early the next morning, the young Rooster flew up to the roof of the barn. He stood there, facing the east.

"I have never done this before," said the Rooster. "I must try my best." He lifted his head and crowed. A weak and scratchy croak was the only sound he was able to make.

The sun did not come up. Clouds covered the sky, and a damp drizzle fell all day. All of the animals of the farm came to the Rooster.

"This is a disaster!" cried a Pig.

"We need our sunshine!" shouted a Sheep.

"Rooster, you must crow much louder," said a Bull. "The sun is ninety-three million miles away. How do you expect it to hear you?"

Very early the next morning, the young Rooster flew up to the roof of the barn again. He took a deep breath, he threw back his head and CROWED. It was the loudest crow that was ever crowed since the beginning of roosters.

The animals on the farm were awakened from their sleep with a start.

"What a noise!" cried a Pig.

"My ears hurt!" shouted the Sheep.

"My head is splitting!" said the Bull.

"I am sorry," said the Rooster, "but I was only doing my job."

He said this with a great deal of pride, for he saw, far to the east, the tip of the morning sun coming up over the trees.

MORAL *A first failure may prepare the way for later success.*

by Jean de la Fontaine • retold by Anne Rockwell

The Dog and the Wolf

One spring day a wolf came out of the forest. He had not had much to eat all winter long and was very hungry. Soon he met a big, strong, handsome dog.

"Good morning, sir," said the wolf to the dog. "You look very happy and well fed. Where have you found food this cold winter?"

"Ah!" said the dog. "I am very fortunate. I do not have to find food. My master feeds me."

The wolf looked suspiciously at the dog. "Hmm," he said. "What do you have to do for this master who feeds you so well?"

"Not much," answered the dog. "I must go for walks with him, and fetch sticks and bring them to him, and sleep in front of the fire by his chair, and be faithful to him, always. I tell you, my friend, it's not at all a bad life. Last night I had roast beef, boiled potatoes, breast of chicken, and a piece of cheese for supper." The dog licked his chops, remembering his good dinner. "Oh, yes," he added, "and I have my own dish to eat from."

"Don't tell me about such delicious things!" cried the wolf. "It makes my stomach growl just to hear you. How fortunate you are!"

"Come with me," said the dog. "You look a little like a dog, and after a good meal and a bath and brushing I am quite sure my master would give you to his servant."

"Oh, how can I thank you?" said the wolf as he loped along beside the dog toward the master's house.

Then the wolf noticed something around the dog's neck that shone in the sun. "What is that you are wearing around your neck?" he asked.

"Oh, that," replied the dog. "That is nothing; it is only my collar."

"And what is a collar? Why do you wear it?" asked the wolf.

"No reason," said the dog. "It is only something my master uses when he chains me up in the yard at night."

"Chains you up!" shouted the wolf. "Do you mean to tell me that you are tied up at night? I love to roam through the forest by moonlight. If I come home with you, would I have to be chained up like you?"

"Of course," answered the dog. "Believe me, that is a small price to pay for all the good things my master gives me. Hurry up, my friend. It is almost time for lunch."

But the wolf did not hear him, for he had run away.

"Chained up all night," muttered the wolf to himself as he ran back to the forest. "I would rather go hungry and have my freedom than be well fed and chained up like that!"

MORAL *All good things come at a price.*

retold by Marie L. McLaughlin

Two Mice

Once there were two prairie mice. The first mouse was hardworking. During harvest each morning, she filled an empty cast-off snakeskin with ground beans, then dragged it home with her teeth.

The other mouse was lazy and careless. She danced around the campfires and talked all night long. By morning, she was too tired to gather beans. When an early frost reminded her that winter was coming, she ran to the other mouse for help.

The hardworking mouse asked, "Where were you during the moon when snakes cast off their skins? You have no bag to gather beans."

The lazy mouse answered, "I was here, but I was busy dancing and talking."

The hardworking mouse gave the lazy mouse a snakeskin and told her to waste no more time. The lazy mouse ran off to gather beans, but winter came so quickly that she went hungry.

MORAL *Work before pleasure makes life better.*

Think and Respond

1. How are the proverbs and fables in this selection alike?

2. Why is it important to read the headings and titles on these pages?

3. What do you think this proverb means: *Working* **persistently,** *ants can fill the nest with food?* Say it in your own words.

4. Which of the proverbs or fables do you think teaches the most important lesson? Explain.

5. As you read the fables in this selection, what reading strategies did you find helpful?

Making Connections

Compare Texts

1 How can proverbs and fables help us grow and learn?

2 What is the difference between a moral and a proverb?

3 Would the proverb *Working persistently, ants can fill the nest with food* make sense as the moral of the fable "Two Mice"? Why or why not? How could you change the proverb to make it fit that fable better?

4 How are the fables "The Hare and the Tortoise" and "Two Mice" alike?

5 Write a proverb that explains a valuable lesson you have learned about life.

Write a Fable

Choose your favorite proverb from "Sayings We Share." Write a short fable based on the proverb, and use the proverb as the moral. Make a story map to plan your fable.

Writing CONNECTION

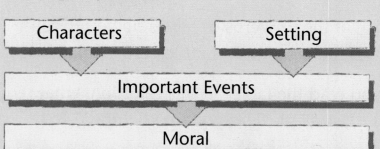

Characters

Setting

Important Events

Moral

Plan a Video

"Two Mice" is a fable of the Sioux people. The Sioux are a Native American people who live on the Great Plains. Research a Native American tribe or nation of your area. Find out about their customs, traditions, and folklore. Plan a video that you could use to share the information you find. Draw pictures to show scenes from the video, and write what the narrator or characters would say.

Make a Display

In "Sayings We Share," you read this African proverb: "As a crab walks, so walk its children." Crabs live in oceans in many parts of the world. Find out more about crabs. How and why are crabs able to survive in so many different places? How many different kinds are there? Set up a display that has pictures, maps, and written facts.

Narrative Elements

Focus Skill

The tortoise in "The Hare and the Tortoise" has a problem. She wants to win a race against the hare, but the hare is much faster than she is.

How does she solve the problem?

While the hare takes a nap, the tortoise keeps going until she passes him and wins the race. These events make up the **plot** of the story.

A story also has a **theme**, or a message that the author wants the reader to understand. The message in "The Hare and the Tortoise" is stated in the moral: *Slow and steady wins the race.*

Often when you read a story or a piece of nonfiction, however, the theme or message is not stated. You have to think about it and figure it out. Ask yourself, "What is the author trying to say?"

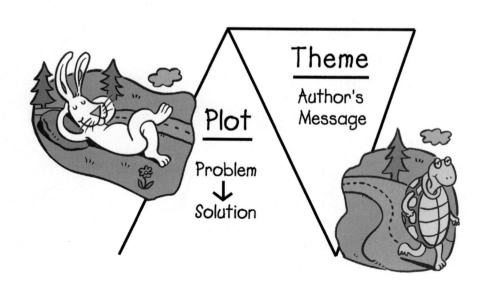

Plot

Problem
↓
Solution

Theme

Author's Message

Visit *The Learning Site!*
www.harcourtschool.com

See *Skills* and *Activities*

Test Prep
Narrative Elements

▶ **Read the story.**

The Donkey and the Songbird

A donkey was hard at work, pulling a heavy load. Suddenly he heard a beautiful song. It came from a tiny songbird perched on a tree. "Oh, Bird," cried the donkey. "Please teach me to sing!"

The songbird knew she could not teach him to sing, but she did not want to hurt his feelings. So she said, "All right, Donkey. I'll teach you to sing if you'll teach me to pull heavy loads."

The donkey laughed. "You can't pull heavy loads. You're much too small!"

"Then I'll be on my way," said the songbird, and off she flew.

Now answer numbers 1 and 2.
Base your answers on the story.

1. **What is the problem in this story? Write a sentence to explain.**

Tip
Think about what may be making one character unhappy.

2. **Which sentence best expresses the theme of the story?**

   A It is better to be strong than to be a good singer.

   B Musical sounds are more pleasant than harsh ones.

   C We all have our own talents.

   D Try not to hurt the feelings of others.

Tip
Reread the story to figure out the author's message.

Writer's Handbook

Contents

Purposes for Writing

There are many different purposes for writing. You might be asked to write **to inform, to respond to something you read, to entertain or express feelings,** or **to persuade.** Sometimes you may write for more than one purpose. For example, when writing a friendly letter, you may write to inform the reader about an event and to express your feelings about the event. Before you write, it is important that you think about the task, the audience, and the purpose for writing. Ask yourself these questions:

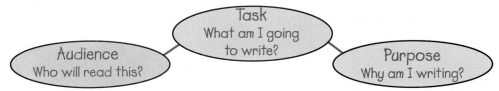

Remember as you are writing to be creative and have fun with your topic. Place yourself in the place of your audience and ask yourself, "What can I write about this topic that will excite my audience?"

Expository Writing

The purpose for expository writing is to inform. This kind of writing explains something. Examples of expository writing are how-to essays, descriptive paragraphs, and research reports.

Sample prompt: *Explain how to get to your house from your school.*

Tips for Expository Writing

- Write a topic sentence that tells the main idea or what you are explaining.
- Organize the information into paragraphs that tell about one idea.
- Use vivid, descriptive language and specific details to convey your interest in the topic to your readers.

Literary Response

When you write to respond to something you have read, your purpose is to show that you understand the passage or selection.

Tips for Literary Response

- Write a topic sentence that answers the question.
- Use your own experience and details from the selection to support your topic sentence.
- Restate your main idea in the conclusion.

Expressive Writing

The purpose for expressive writing is to share your feelings or to entertain. Sometimes expressive writing describes something. Examples of expressive writing are personal narratives, stories, and poems.

Sample prompt: *There are many things to do on a rainy day. Think about what you would do on a rainy day. Now write a story about what you did on a rainy day.*

Tips for Expressive Writing

- Introduce yourself or your characters.
- Use your personal voice to describe what you are writing about.
- Include as many details about what you or your characters see, hear, touch, taste, and smell to draw your reader into the story.
- Have an ending that makes sense.

Persuasive Writing

The purpose of persuasive writing is to persuade readers to agree with your opinions or to take action.

Sample prompt: *Imagine that you want to convince your parents to let you have a sleep over. Write a persuasive paragraph that gives reasons why having a sleep over is a good idea.*

Tips for Persuasive Writing

- Have an interesting beginning that explains your opinion.
- Give at least three reasons why you feel the way you do.
- In your conclusion, restate your opinion or ask your reader to take action.

Try This

What would be the purpose for each of these kinds of writing: a telephone message, a joke, a recipe, and an advertisement?

The Writing Process

The writing process has five steps. You will go back and forth through these steps as you write.

Prewriting: In this step, you plan what you will write. Identify your purpose and who your audience is. Then choose a topic and organize your information.

Drafting: Write out your ideas in sentences and paragraphs. Follow your prewriting plan.

Revising: Make changes to make your writing easier to understand or more interesting to read.

Proofreading: In this step, check for errors in grammar, spelling, capitalization, and punctuation. Then make a final copy of your work.

Publishing: Choose a way to share your work. You may add pictures or read your writing aloud.

Here is an example, showing how Keesha used the writing process to write a personal narrative.

Prewriting

Keesha was asked to write a personal narrative. Her audience would be her classmates. She remembered the time she broke her leg. Her next step was to write down everything she could remember.

> Fell off bicycle.
> Broke leg.
> Got crutches.
> Couldn't get out of a chair.
> Couldn't go up and down stairs.
> Then learned how to go really
>   fast on them.

Drafting

Keesha wrote about the events in the order that they took place. She also thought about details that would describe what happened.

Revising

Keesha made changes to improve her writing. She checked to see whether her ideas were in the right order. She added details and took out unnecessary information. She made a run-on sentence into two separate sentences. Here is her first draft with some changes she made in **blue.**

Proofreading

Keesha looked for mistakes in grammar, spelling, punctuation, and capitalization. The corrections in **red** show the changes she made while proofreading.

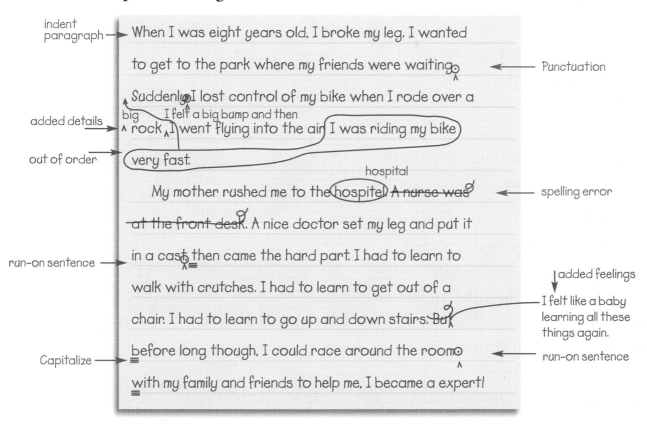

Publishing

Keesha decided to read her story aloud to the class. She brought her crutches to school. She showed how hard it was to get out of a chair. Then she answered questions.

Try This

Imagine you are writing a story about a time you tried something new. Decide what your purpose and audience will be. Then think of interesting ways to publish your story.

How to Get Ideas

Once you know your purpose and audience, here are ways to get ideas:

Keep **lists** in a Reading log or idea bank.

- **Think about things you like to do.**

Things I Like
arts and crafts
sports
board games
reading

- **Think about subjects you like in school.**

Interesting Lessons in School
air pressure experiment
estimation games
mock trial in social studies

- **Research people, places, and things you want to know more about.**

Things I want to learn more about
weather forecasting
Paris, France
Video games
art programs on the computer

Keep a **timeline** of interesting things that happen in your life.

- Record feelings and experiences in a personal journal.

- Draw pictures to remind you of memorable events.

- Describe yourself at different times in your life.

Use **freewriting** when you get stuck.

- Start with a topic word or a feeling word.

- Write freely for several minutes. Do not pick your pencil up off the paper.

- Write every thought that comes to your mind. You never know when a good idea will come to you.

When you find an idea you want to write about, you can explore it some more, using an idea web. Janna made a web like this one to describe an elephant that she saw at the zoo.

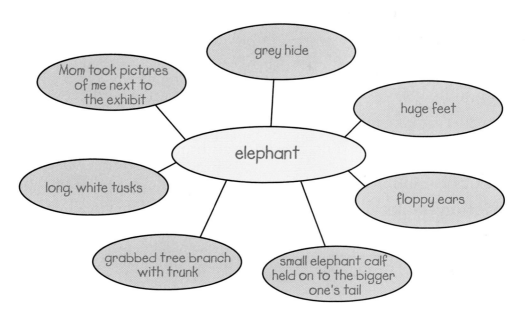

Guidelines for Making an Idea Web:

- Write a word as your starting point. Circle it.

- Around it, write ideas that pop into your head.

- Circle each idea.

Try This

Select an object that is important to you. Imagine that you will write a paragraph about it. Make a web like the web Janna made, but write your object in the center circle. In the outside circles, write all your ideas about the object.

Library Resources

You can find books, magazines, videos, audiocassettes, and even games in a library. The library lends all of these items free to the people who live in the area. All you need to do is ask for a library card.

The books in a library are arranged so that you can find what you need easily. **Fiction books** are arranged in alphabetical order by the last names of the authors. **Nonfiction books** are grouped according to subject. **Reference books** such as dictionaries, atlases, almanacs, and encyclopedias, can be found in a special section of the library.

Libraries have card catalogs to help you find books. A card catalog has a card for every book in the library. These cards are put in alphabetical order in drawers. An **electronic card catalog** has the same information, but it is on a computer.

At the computer, you can type **keywords,** such as the name of an author, the title of a book, or the subject of a book. Then the computer will provide a list of titles. Each **entry,** or listing, includes a short summary of the book.

J974.45.C
Chandler, Timothy.
Pioneer Life in America.
Nonfic.
Children's Room
©1990

A close look at the everyday life of pioneers in this country

J971.04F
Fellers, Frances.
Life in the West. Nonfic.
Children's Room
©1994

Struggles of the early settlers in America's Western states

Using a Dictionary

A **dictionary** is a book that gives the meanings of words. It also shows how to say them.

Words in a dictionary are listed in alphabetical order. At the top of each dictionary page are **guide words.** The first guide word is the first word on the page. The next guide word is the last word on the page. Use the guide words to help you find the page that lists the word you need.

A **pronunciation key** can be found on every other page. The key shows the letters and symbols used in the pronunciation of each entry. Then it gives sample words to show how to pronounce each sound.

> The words in dark type on each dictionary page are called **entry words.**

> The special spelling shows how to say the word aloud. The way a word sounds when it is said aloud is called its **pronunciation.**

> The letter or letters after the pronunciation tell the **part of speech.** Most dictionaries use abbreviations for this.

> The meaning of a word is called the **definition.** When a word has more than one definition, the definitions are numbered. The most common definition comes first.

gav • el [gav' əl] *n.* A small wooden mallet used by a person in charge of a meeting to call for attention or order.
ga • votte [gə vot'] *n.* A 17th-century French dance, like the minuet but somewhat quicker.
Ga • wain [gä' win] *n.* One of the knights of the Round Table, nephew of King Arthur.
gawk [gôk] *informal* **1** *v.* To stare stupidly; gape. **2** *n.* An awkward, clumsy person.
gawk • y [gô 'kē] *adj.* **gawk • i • er, gawk • i • est** Awkward or clumsy. —**gawk' i • ly** *adv.* —**gawk' i • ness** *n.*
gaze [gāz] *v.* **gazed, gaz • ing,** *n.* **1** *v.* To look steadily; stare. **2** *n.* A steady or fixed look. —**gaz' er** *n.*

a	at	i	it	oŏ	book	oi	oil
ā	ape	ī	ice	ōō	cool	ou	out
â	care	o	odd	u	up	ng	long
ä	father	ō	old	û	burn	th	thin
e	end	ô	order	yōō	use	ŧħ	this
ē	equal					zh	vision
ə = a in *above*		e in *taken*		i in *pencil*		o in *lemon*	u in *circus*

Pronunciation Key

Try This

Play a game with a friend where you each race to look up the same word in a dictionary. The person who writes the word, the page number, and the guide words first wins.

Using a Thesaurus

A **thesaurus** is a book that lists words and their synonyms and antonyms.

Synonyms are words that have almost the same meanings. **Antonyms** are words with opposite meanings. **Entry words** are listed in alphabetical order. **Guide words** at the top of each page show the first and last words on that page.

A thesaurus is an important tool because it can help you choose the right word to use.

The word **broken** is an **entry word.** Entry words are in dark type. They are listed in alphabetical order in the thesaurus.

The abbreviation *adj.* tells the part of speech.
Abbreviations

n.	noun	*v.*	verb
adj.	adjective	*adv.*	adverb
prep.	preposition		

broken *adj.* Not in good condition; not working; damaged: The *broken* cup lay in many pieces.

cracked Broken but not completely falling apart: The *cracked* mirror still hung on the wall.

crushed Broken completely by being pressed between two things: A *crushed* tomato was at the bottom of the grocery bag.

ANTONYMS: fixed, mended, repaired

These are **synonyms** for the word *broken*. Read each definition to find the word that has the best meaning for you.

Using an Atlas

An **atlas** is a book of maps. A world atlas has maps of every country in the world. Some atlases have maps of only one country. Different kinds of maps show different facts about places.

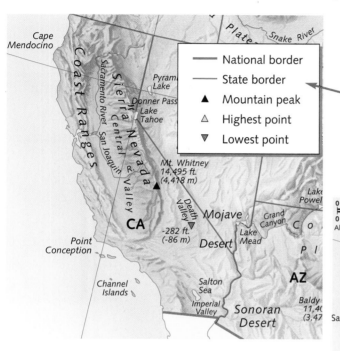

This is a *relief* map. It shows where in California there are mountains, valleys, and bodies of water. Colors are used to show how high the land is. The **legend** tells you what the symbols mean.

This map shows the names of some cities in California. The legend, or **map key,** tells you that the city with a star next to its name is the state capital. On the map, the star is next to Sacramento, the capital of California.

Try This

Look in an atlas for other maps of California with different information than the maps shown here. What types of information do they present? What might the information on those maps be useful for? Make a list of the different types of maps you find and what they might be useful for.

Book Parts

Books are organized to help you find information.

Front of the Book

- The **title page** shows the name of the book, the author, and the name of the company that made, or published, the book. It also says where the book was published.

- The **copyright page** tells you in what year the book was made.

- The **table of contents** lists the names of the chapters or units. It tells on which page each chapter or unit begins.

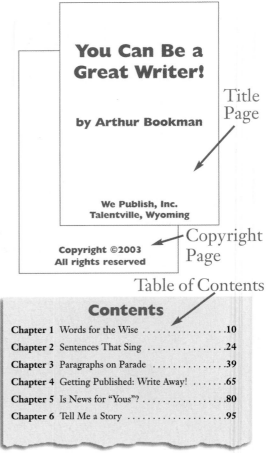

Title Page

Copyright Page

Table of Contents

Contents

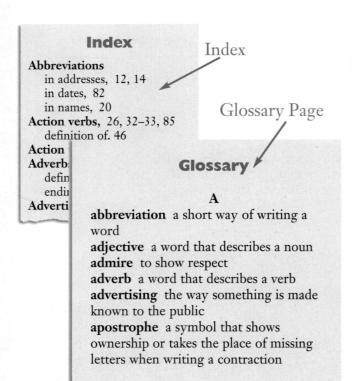

Index

Glossary Page

Back of the Book

- The **glossary** gives the meanings of important words in the book. The glossary is arranged in alphabetical order.

- The **index** is a list of topics in the book. Page numbers next to each word tell where in the book you can find that information.

Using an Encyclopedia

An **encyclopedia** is a book or a set of books that gives information about many different subjects. In a printed set of encyclopedias, each **volume,** or book, has one or more letters on its spine (or side). The letters go from A to Z. Sometimes each book has a number as well. A CD-ROM version of a printed encyclopedia will sometimes have all the information from all the volumes on one disc!

All the subjects in any kind of encyclopedia are arranged in alphabetical order. If you wanted to look up ponds in a printed encyclopedia, you would look in volume 8, *P.*

Articles give facts about the topics in an encyclopedia.

This **guide word** tells you the last topic on this page.

Pony

Pond is a small, quiet body of water that is shallow enough for sunlight to reach the bottom. The sunlight allows plants to grow across the bottom of the pond, from shore to shore. In most cases, ponds are the home for many kinds of animals and plants. The wind and streams carry in eggs and seeds that grow into different forms of life. Pond animals include birds, fish, frogs, insects and turtles. Many ponds have plants that grow under the water and leafy plants that float on top of it.
See also **Marsh; Swamp**

Cross-references tell you where to find articles on a similar topic.

Try This

Look up a keyword in a CD-ROM encyclopedia and in a print encyclopedia. Which do you think gives more information? Which do you prefer to use? Why?

Organizing Information

Note Taking

A good way to remember information you read is to **take notes.** You can look at your notes when you write a report or study for a test.

Putting your notes on cards can help you organize ideas and details. Make a separate card for each main idea. Then you will be able to put the cards in order in different ways if you need to. This can be useful if you are writing a report.

> On the card, write the **title** and **name of the author** of the book where you found the information you will use. If possible, include the **page numbers**.

> Write the **main idea** as a heading on the card. It may help to write the main idea as a question.

Lorrie Lindstrom, All About Ants, pages 54-64

What kinds of ants are there?

1. army ants—travel, hunt

2. Amazon ants—slave makers

3. honey ants—juices

4. leaf-cutter ants—leaves above heads

> Under the main idea write **details**. Use only enough words to help you remember the important facts.

Note Taking with Graphic Organizers

Sometimes it helps to use a graphic organizer when you take notes. A **K-W-L** chart is a good chart for note taking. The chart has three columns.

- Write what you **know** about the subject in the **K** column. Do this before you read.

- Write questions about what you **want** to find out in the **W** column.

- Write what you **learn** in the **L** column. Do this as you are reading.

Ants		
K	W	L
small black or red insects	What kinds of ants are there?	army ants: travel most of the time
live in large groups	What is special about each kind?	Amazon ants: kidnap other ants
very strong		honey ants: collect juice

A **web** is another helpful graphic organizer to use when you are taking notes. A web shows how facts or ideas are connected.

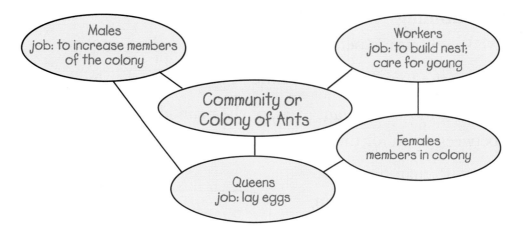

A **Venn diagram** helps you compare two things. This Venn diagram shows how ants and termites are alike and how they are different.

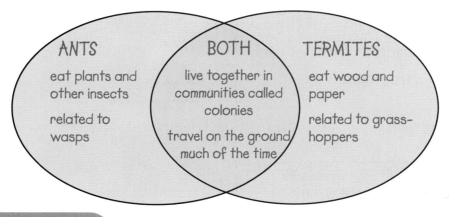

Try This

Think about two of your favorite things to do during your free time. On a sheet of paper, make a Venn diagram and use it to compare and contrast these two activities.

Outlining

Outlining is a good way to organize information. When you read, an outline can help you keep track of the main ideas and the details in an article or book. When you write, an outline can help you plan your ideas into paragraphs.

Tips for Outlining

- Make an outline before you write.

- Write the topic of your outline at the top as its title.

- List the most important ideas, or the main ideas. Leave space between them for the details.

- Put a Roman numeral followed by a period in front of each main idea.

- List supporting details below each main idea.

- Put a capital letter followed by a period in front of each supporting detail.

This outline uses questions for main ideas and words and phrases for supporting details. You can also create a **sentence outline** in which all the items are complete sentences.

The Moon

I. What is a moon?
 A. a satellite that orbits a planet
 B. Earth's one satellite
II. What does a moon look like?
 A. rocky and gray
 B. high mountains
 C. craters
III. What is it like on Earth's moon?
 A. no air
 B. black sky
 C. temperature
  1. very hot
  2. very cold
 D. little gravity

Here is a report about the moon that was written using the outline. Compare the outline and the report.

The Moon

Since ancient times, people have told stories and sung songs about the moon. In fact, a moon is something in space that circles around, or orbits, a planet. Some planets have twenty moons or more. Earth has just one.

The first paragraph explains **what a moon is.**

The surface of the moon is rocky and gray. It is covered with a layer of fine dust. On the moon, you can see high mountains. Many of these were volcanoes at one time. There are also craters, or holes, on the moon. Some craters are less than one foot across. Other craters are as much as seven hundred miles across. Flying masses of space matter, called meteorites, probably crashed into the moon and made these craters.

The second paragraph explains **how the moon looks.**

A visit to the moon would be a strange experience! There is no air, or atmosphere, on the moon. That means sound cannot travel. On the moon, the sky is always black. Even during the day you can see the stars. The temperature on the moon is very hot or very cold. One place has temperatures above the boiling point of water. Another place has temperatures hundreds of degrees below zero. Finally, the pull of gravity is much less on the moon. If you weigh 90 pounds on Earth, you will weigh only 15 pounds on the moon. Just think how high you could jump!

The third paragraph explains **what it is like to be on the moon.**

Try This

Make an outline of what you do on a Saturday or Sunday. Divide the outline into three main sections. List at least 2 supporting details under each main idea. Remember to use Roman numerals and letters to separate the different parts of your outline.

Traits of Good Writing

Writing is like any other skill or activity. It takes time, practice, and effort. There are rules you have to learn and **traits,** or features, of good writing that you will learn to recognize. But once you understand those rules and traits, writing can be a lot of fun. Think about another activity you enjoy. When you did it for the first few times, learning the rules was important. Once you knew the rules, though, you could focus on having fun.

Think about drawing, for example. To draw well, an artist needs to be able to imagine what he wants to draw, sketch it out on whatever he's drawing on, and then add details and maybe colors to make the drawing look real. Very few people can do this well from the beginning. Most artists have to train their imaginations to see things in detail, and train their hands to make the marks and shapes that look like what they're imagining. Creating mental images, sketching, and detail drawing are **traits of good drawing.** They are skills that good artists practice and improve in order to draw well.

Good writing takes practice at these skills, too. This web shows the **traits of good writing.**

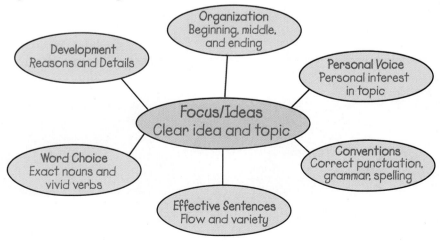

Quick Checklist for Good Writers

Good writers practice, practice, practice! As you practice, ask yourself these questions. If you can say "yes" to most of them, you are doing quite well indeed! If you need work in some areas, use the lessons in this handbook. Keep practicing!

✔ **FOCUS/IDEAS** Are my ideas clear? Do I stay on the topic?

✔ **ORGANIZATION** Do I have a clear beginning, middle, and ending? Are similar ideas grouped together in paragraphs?

✔ **DEVELOPMENT** Do I use details and reasons to support my ideas?

✔ **VOICE** Do I seem to care about my topic?

✔ **EFFECTIVE SENTENCES** Do I use a variety of sentence types?

✔ **WORD CHOICE** Do I use exact nouns and vivid verbs?

✔ **CONVENTIONS** Are my spelling, grammar, and punctuation correct?

Try This

Choose a piece of writing from your portfolio. Use the Quick Checklist. What are your strengths? What can you improve? Jot down your ideas in your Writer's Journal.

Using a Rubric

A rubric is a list you can use to check your writing. It spells out the main points of good writing.

Before writing   Use the list to remind you of the traits of good writing.

During writing   Use the list to see how you can improve your drafts.

After writing   Use the list to see if your essay or story has all the points of good writing.

Here is a checklist you can use to self-evaluate your writing.

My Best Score

✔ Do I make the topic and my ideas clear to the reader?

✔ Does my essay move from beginning to the middle to the end smoothly? Is it easy to follow?

✔ Do I support my ideas with specific reasons and details?

✔ Do my words show my interest and knowledge in the topic?

✔ Do I use different kinds of sentences in my essay?

✔ Are my choices of nouns and verbs specific and vivid?

✔ Do I use correct grammar, spelling, and punctuation?

Peer Conferences

You can make your writing better by reading your work to a classmate. **Peer conferences** are a good way to get helpful comments and suggestions.

Here are some questions to ask a friend when you want help with your writing:

1. Is my topic interesting to you? Can you figure out my point of view?

2. Do you understand the order of events? Is there anything I left out?

3. Is this detail important? Should I include it?

4. Can you suggest a better word for_____?

5. Do I have any choppy sentences? Can any sentences be combined?

6. Do I have any run-on sentences?

7. Are there mistakes in spelling, grammar, or punctuation?

Tips for peer conferences:

- Listen carefully to someone else's writing.

- Make suggestions, but don't tell the writer what to do.

- Remember to tell what you like about the writing.

- Be polite and encouraging. Agree or disagree in a pleasant way.

Try This

Write a paragraph about a time you went somewhere new and had a good time. Share your paragraph with a partner, and conduct a peer conference.

Giving an Oral Presentation

One way to share your writing with classmates is to give an oral presentation.

Tips for giving an oral presentation:

1. Write the report on note cards in big print.
2. Practice reading your report aloud in front of a mirror or to a friend.
3. When you speak, look at your audience some of the time. Make motions with your hands, too. This will keep your listeners interested in your presentation.
4. Speak clearly and loudly enough for everyone to hear you. Speak slowly enough for everyone to understand you. Change your tone of voice every now and then to stress important parts of what you read.
5. Make your presentation more interesting by using props. You might use things that describe your topic, such as posters, pictures or charts.
6. When you finish, ask for questions from the audience.

Tips for listeners:

1. Listen politely to the speaker's presentation. Don't talk with your neighbors.
2. Look at the speaker to show your interest.
3. Save your questions for the end. You may also want to add information you have on the topic that might be interesting.

Giving a Multimedia Presentation

You can use different means of communication, such as pictures, videos, music, or drama, when you share a report with your class. This is called a **multimedia presentation.** Here are the steps to follow:

1. Decide which multimedia aids fit your report best. For example, if you are doing a report on state songs, you might bring a CD or cassette tape of music. If you are doing a report on tropical fish, you might bring photos, drawings, videotapes, or maps.

2. Get permission to use equipment that you need, such as a tape recorder or a videotape player. Learn how to operate the equipment ahead of time. If you are presenting your report as a play or skit, ask classmates to assist you by acting out parts.

3. Decide at what time during your presentation you will use the multimedia aids.

4. Organize the spoken part of your presentation. Write notes of what you will say. Practice reading your notes.

5. Invite your classmates to ask questions about your report.

Try This

Imagine that you have been asked to give an oral report about a hobby that you have or a club in which you are involved. Make a list of aids you could use in your presentation.

Using the Glossary

Like a dictionary, this glossary lists words in alphabetical order. To find a word, look it up by its first letter or letters.

To save time, use the **guide words** at the top of each page. These show you the first and last words on the page. Look at the guide words to see if your word falls between them alphabetically.

Here is an example of a glossary entry:

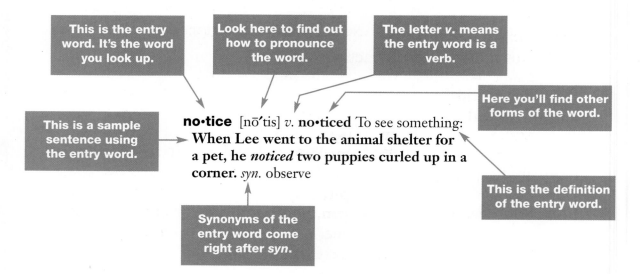

This is the entry word. It's the word you look up.

Look here to find out how to pronounce the word.

The letter *v.* means the entry word is a verb.

Here you'll find other forms of the word.

This is a sample sentence using the entry word.

no·tice [nō′tis] *v.* **no·ticed** To see something: **When Lee went to the animal shelter for a pet, he *noticed* two puppies curled up in a corner.** *syn.* observe

This is the definition of the entry word.

Synonyms of the entry word come right after *syn.*

Word Origins

Throughout the glossary, you will find notes about word origins, or how words get started and change. Words often have interesting backgrounds that can help you remember what they mean.

Here is an example of a word origin note:

familiar At first, *familiar* meant "of the family," from the Latin word *familiaris*. Its meaning grew to include friends and to become "known from being around often." *Familiar* began to be used in English in the 1300s.

Pronunciation

The pronunciation in brackets is a respelling that shows how the word is pronounced.

The **pronunciation key** explains what the symbols in a respelling mean. A shortened pronunciation key appears on every other page of the glossary.

PRONUNCIATION KEY*

a	add, map	m	move, seem	u	up, done
ā	ace, rate	n	nice, tin	û(r)	burn, term
â(r)	care, air	ng	ring, song	yo͞o	fuse, few
ä	palm, father	o	odd, hot	v	vain, eve
b	bat, rub	ō	open, so	w	win, away
ch	check, catch	ô	order, jaw	y	yet, yearn
d	dog, rod	oi	oil, boy	z	zest, muse
e	end, pet	ou	pout, now	zh	vision, pleasure
ē	equal, tree	o͝o	took, full	ə	the schwa, an
f	fit, half	o͞o	pool, food		unstressed vowel
g	go, log	p	pit, stop		representing the
h	hope, hate	r	run, poor		sound spelled
i	it, give	s	see, pass		*a* in *above*
ī	ice, write	sh	sure, rush		*e* in *sicken*
j	joy, ledge	t	talk, sit		*i* in *possible*
k	cool, take	th	thin, both		*o* in *melon*
l	look, rule	t̶h̶	this, bathe		*u* in *circus*

Other symbols:
- • separates words into syllables
- ′ indicates heavier stress on a syllable
- ′ indicates light stress on a syllable

Abbreviations: *adj.* adjective, *adv.* adverb, *conj.* conjunction, *interj.* interjection, *n.* noun, *prep.* preposition, *pron.* pronoun, *syn.* synonym, *v.* verb

* The Pronunciation Key, adapted entries, and the Short Key that appear on the following pages are reprinted from *HBJ School Dictionary* Copyright © 1990 by Harcourt Brace & Company. Reprinted by permission of Harcourt Brace & Company.

A

ac·ci·dent [ak′sə•dənt] *n.* An event that happens without warning, sometimes causing harm or damage: **Pedro broke his arm in an *accident*.**

aim [ām] *v.* **aimed** To point an object at a target: **Carol *aimed* the soccer ball at the goal.**

aim

anc·ient [ān′shənt] *adj.* Very old: **The *ancient* rock formed a long time ago.**

ap·point·ment [ə•point′mənt] *n.* A time to be somewhere or to meet someone: **Laronda was on time for her *appointment* with the dentist.**

ap·proach [ə•prōch′] *v.* To come closer to; to move toward: **As you *approach* the music room, you will hear the band playing.**

as·sis·tant [ə•sis′tənt] *n.* A person who helps: **The cook's *assistant* stirred the soup.**

at·ten·tion [ə•ten′shən] *n.* The act of noticing, listening to, or thinking about someone or something: **Pay *attention* to cars, bicycles, and traffic signals when you cross the street.**

au·di·ence [ô′dē•əns] *n.* A group of people watching and listening to a performance: **The *audience* clapped until Aretha sang another song.**

⌐ Word Origins

audience The word *audience* comes from the Latin word *audire*, meaning "to hear." An audience hears when something is read or spoken out loud. This word came into the English language in the 1300s.

B

ball·hawk [bôl′hôk] *n.* A nickname given to a ballplayer who is good at catching balls, especially ones that are hard to catch: **When Joey made another amazing catch, his teammates began to call him a *ballhawk*.**

be·yond [bē•yond′] *prep.* Outside of; farther away than: **Dad told me not to ride my bike *beyond* the corner of our street.**

bil·lion [bil′yən] *n.* **bil·lions** A thousand million; an amount that seems too great to count or know: **There are *billions* of grains of sand on the beach.**

brunch [brunch] *n.* A meal that combines breakfast and lunch: **That restaurant serves *brunch* from 11:00 A.M. until 2:00 P.M. every Sunday.**

C

cap·tain [kap′tən] *n.* A person who leads or commands: **The *captain* led her softball team to victory.**

cart·wheel
[kärt′(h)wēl′] *n.* A sideways movement in which the body turns like a wheel: **You need good balance to turn a *cartwheel* without falling over.**

cartwheel

case [kās] *n.* A problem that a detective tries to solve: **Police officers will uncover the facts of this robbery *case*.**

cer·e·mo·ny [ser′ə·mō′nē] *n.* **cer·e·mo·nies** A formal action performed in a set way: **The graduation *ceremonies* are held here every year.**

col·lapse [kə·laps′] *v.* **col·lapsed** To fall down from being very tired, hot, or sick: **After running the last part of the race at full speed, Sara *collapsed* just after crossing the finish line.**

col·lec·tion [kə·lek′shən] *n.* Things gathered together for study or as a hobby: **Jake has put together a *collection* of different marbles.**

com·fort [kum′fərt] *n.* Someone or something that makes others feel better when they are in pain or unhappy: **Terry played with the younger children and was a *comfort* to them while their mother was away.**

com·fort·a·ble [kum′fər·tə·bəl] *adj.* At ease: **Roland felt *comfortable* in his aunt's house.** *syn.* content

com·mand [kə·mand′] *n.* **com·mands** An order to do something: **When the captain shouted *commands*, the soldiers quickly did what they were told.**

com·pete [kəm·pēt′] *v.* To take part in a contest: **Lisa will *compete* in the race.**

con·cen·trate [kon′sən·trāt′] *v.* To give complete attention to; to think hard about: **It was hard to *concentrate* on the test because of the noise from the playground.**

con·fi·dent [kon′fə·dənt] *adj.* Sure of something: **Ramon was *confident* that he had done well on the math test.** *syn.* certain

con·ta·gious [kən·tā′jəs] *adj.* Spread easily from one person to another; usually used to describe a disease: **Many people get the flu because it is very *contagious*.**

crea·ture [krē′chər] *n.* Any living being; an animal or person: **Some people think a spider is a scary *creature*.**

creatures

cu·ri·ous [kyŏŏr′ē·əs] *adj.* Full of questions about things and wanting to know the answers: **If you're so *curious* about what's inside the box, open it and find out.** *syn.* interested

D

dart [därt] *v.* **dart·ed** To move quickly and suddenly: **The scared rabbit *darted* into its hole when it saw me coming.**

a add	e end	o odd	$\overline{oo}$ pool	oi oil	th this	a in *above*
ā ace	ē equal	ō open	u up	ou pout	zh vision	e in *sicken*
â care	i it	ô order	û burn	ng ring		ə = { i in *possible*
ä palm	ī ice	ŏŏ took	yōō fuse	th thin		o in *melon*
						u in *circus*

def·i·nite·ly [def′ə·nit·lē] *adv.* In a plain and clear way: **That color is *definitely* purple.**

del·i·cate [del′ə·kit] *adj.* Easily broken or damaged; needing to be treated with care: **The *delicate* hand-painted eggs were placed in special holders.** *syns.* weak; fragile

de·part·ment [di·pärt′mənt] *n.* A part or section of a government or a company with members who have special duties: **A man from the fire *department* spoke to the students about fire safety.**

de·pend [di·pend′] *v.* To trust or count on someone to do something: **You can *depend* on us to clean up after the party.**

de·tec·tive [di·tek′tiv] *n.* A person who investigates or finds hidden information: **The *detective* found clues and solved the mystery.**

drift [drift] *n.* **drifts** A large pile of something, such as snow, that is formed by the wind: **During the blizzard, the wind blew the snow into *drifts* as high as twelve feet.**

ea·ger [ē′gər] *adj.* Full of excited interest: **Zoey was so *eager* to see the newborn kittens that she ran all the way home.**

earn [ûrn] *v.* **earned** To gain through effort: **Patrick *earned* his allowance by cleaning his bedroom.**

en·joy [in·joi′] *v.* **en·joy·ing** To get happiness from: **You can tell by their happy faces that the girls are *enjoying* the party.**

e·quip·ment [i·kwip′mənt] *n.* Things used for a special purpose: **The new store sells skates, balls, helmets, and other sports *equipment*.** *syn.* supplies

e·rupt [i·rupt′] *v.* **e·rupt·ing** To break out with force, as lava does from a volcano: **The photographs of the volcano *erupting* in a fiery explosion were amazing.**

erupt

es·cape [i·skāp′] *v.* To get free or get away from danger: **The animals were able to *escape* from the forest fire.** *syn.* flee

Word Origins

escape What does taking off one's coat have to do with escaping? *Escape* comes from the Latin word *excappāre*, which first meant "to take off one's cape or coat." By the time the word came into English, it meant "to throw off something that holds one back, or to gain one's freedom."

ex·plode [ik·splōd′] *v.* **ex·plod·ed** To burst out suddenly and with noise: **Jess *exploded* and yelled at the cat when it knocked a vase off the table.**

ex·pres·sion [ik·spresh′ən] *n.* The tone of voice or look on the face that shows a person's feelings: **Tyrone's *expression* made it clear that he thought the joke was funny.**

faith·ful [fāth′fəl] *adj.* Firm and constant; worthy of trust: **A *faithful* friend always keeps a promise.**

fa·mil·iar [fə·mil′yər] *adj.* Well known from having been seen or heard many times: **The band played *familiar* tunes, and everyone sang along.**

Word Origins

familiar At first, *familiar* meant "of the family," from the Latin word *familiaris*. Its meaning grew to include friends and to become "known from being around often." *Familiar* began to be used in English in the 1300s.

fas·ten [fas′ən] *v.* **fas·tened** To attach one thing to another: **Fred *fastened* the long tail to his mouse costume with a safety pin.** *syn.* secure

fault [fôlt] *n.* Guilt or responsibility for doing something wrong: **Juan said it was his *fault* that the dog got out, because he left the gate open.** *syn.* blame

firm [fûrm] *adj.* Not giving in: **Elena's teacher was *firm* about the rules in her class.** *syns.* unchanging; strict

for·tu·nate [fôr′chə·nit] *adj.* Having good luck: **You are *fortunate* to have found your lost wallet.**

gen·er·a·tion [jen·ə·rā′shən] *n.* Any group of people born at about the same time: **My mother is part of a different *generation* than mine.**

glance [glans] *v.* **glanced** To look at very quickly: **Pete *glanced* at the sign on the door as he hurried past.**

grum·ble [grum′bəl] *n.* A low, rumbling sound muttered in complaint: **Surprisingly, Susan did her chores without a *grumble*.**

guide [gīd] *v.* **guid·ed** To show someone the way to go: **The park ranger *guided* the lost hikers out of the woods.** *syn.* lead

gym [jim] *n.* (shortened form of *gymnasium*) A large room or building used for sports and for training athletes: **On Saturday mornings, basketball practice was held in the school *gym*.**

gym

host [hōst] *n.* One who entertains or welcomes guests: **We thanked our *host*, Mr. Morris, for inviting us to spend a day on his farm.**

Word Origins

host If you are a guest in someone's home, that person is your host. Today, *host* and *guest* are words that make you think of a friendly relationship. These two words are also related in an unusual way. They both come from the Latin word *hostis*, which meant "stranger" or "enemy!"

a	add	e	end	o	odd	o͞o	pool	oi	oil	t͟h	this
ā	ace	ē	equal	ō	open	u	up	ou	pout	zh	vision
â	care	i	it	ô	order	û	burn	ng	ring	
ä	palm	ī	ice	o͝o	took	yo͞o	fuse	th	thin	

ə = {
a in *above*
e in *sicken*
i in *possible*
o in *melon*
u in *circus*
}

il·lu·mi·nate [i·lōō′mə·nāt′] *v.*
il·lu·mi·nat·ed To light up: **The flashlight** *illuminated* **the dark stairway.**

lan·guage [lang′gwij] *n.* **lan·guag·es** The words used by a certain group to speak and write: **People from France and Germany speak different** *languages.*

la·va [lä′və or lav′ə] *n.* Hot melted rock that pours out of the mouth of a volcano when it erupts: **When the volcano erupted, red-hot** *lava* **flowed down, covering the empty village.**

lava

lit·ter [lit′ər] *n.* Trash that has been dropped on the ground and left there: **We filled trash bags with the paper cups and other** *litter* **people left along the parade route.**

long [lông] *v.* **longed** To want something very much: **By the end of summer camp, Amy** *longed* **to see her family.** *syn.* desire

ma·rine [mə·rēn′] *adj.* Having to do with the sea: **The scientist went scuba diving to collect** *marine* **plants for his research project.**

med·al [med′əl] *n.*
med·als An award given to winners in sports or other events: **Jean finished first in both contests and won two first-place** *medals.*

medals

mes·sage [mes′ij] *n.* Information passed on to a person by written words or by sound: **While we were out, Susan left a** *message* **on our telephone answering machine.**

mon·i·tor [mon′ə·tər] *n.* A person who watches over something: **The park** *monitor* **will let us in and out of the play area.**

mum·ble [mum′bəl] *v.* **mum·bled** To speak unclearly, with the lips partly closed: **I couldn't understand him when he** *mumbled.*

mus·tache [mus′tash *or* məs·tash′] *n.* The trimmed hair on a man's upper lip: **Grandpa's gray** *mustache* **curves down around the sides of his mouth.**

mustache

Word Origins
mustache *Mustache* came into English from the French in the 1500s. The French word came from the Italian *mostaccio*, which came from the Greek *mystax*, meaning "upper lip."

no•tice [nō′tis] *v.* **no•ticed** To see something: **When Lee went to the animal shelter for a pet, he *noticed* two puppies curled up in a corner.** *syn.* observe

o•bey [ō•bā′] *v.* **o•beys** To do what one is told to do: **Our dog *obeys* all our orders, but our cat won't do anything we tell her to do.**

om•e•let [om′lit] *n.* Eggs that have been beaten and cooked, sometimes with other foods: **The chef beat two eggs and added cheese and mushrooms as he cooked my *omelet*.**

Word Origins

omelet The omelet was named for its thin flat shape. The word *omelet* comes from the 15th-century French word *amalette*, having a meaning similar to "thin plate."

out•field•er [out′fēl′dər] *n.* A ballplayer who catches in the outfield, the area outside of the baseball diamond: **John's hit would have been a home run if the *outfielder* had not caught the ball.**

outfielder

pa•tient•ly [pā′shənt•lē] *adv.* Without fussing or complaining, even after a long time: **The child sat *patiently* for an hour until it was her turn to see the doctor.**

peace•ful [pēs′fəl] *adj.* Calm and quiet: **When the excitement of the parade was over, our street was *peaceful* once again.**

Word Origins

peaceful *Peace*, the base word of *peaceful*, comes from the Latin word *pax*, having a meaning similar to "fixed in place" or "safe." There are many English words that are related to *pax*, such as *pact*, *pacific*, and *pay*.

per•form [pər•fôrm′] *v.* To sing, dance, act, play a musical instrument, or use some other talent in front of an audience: **For the show, Leah will *perform* a song she wrote herself.**

perform

per•sis•tent•ly [pər•sis′tənt•lē] *adv.* Never giving up: **Lance called me *persistently* until he got an answer.**

pos•i•tive [poz′ə•tiv] *adj.* Completely certain or convinced: **Carol is *positive* that she heard a noise.**

pre•fer [pri•fûr′] *v.* To favor or choose one thing over another: **On warm, sunny days my sister and I *prefer* walking to school to taking the bus.**

a add	e end	o odd	o͞o pool	oi oil	th this
ā ace	ē equal	ō open	u up	ou pout	zh vision
â care	i it	ô order	û burn	ng ring	
ä palm	ī ice	o͝o took	yo͞o fuse	th thin	

ə = {
a in *above*
e in *sicken*
i in *possible*
o in *melon*
u in *circus*
}

pre·scrip·tion [pri·skrip′shən] *n.* Written instructions from a doctor for the preparation and use of a medicine: **Dr. Chen wrote a** *prescription* **for medicine to clear up Amy's ear infection.**

pre·tend [pri·tend′] *v.* **pre·tend·ed** To make believe: **Diane did not want to answer her sister's questions, so she** *pretended* **to be asleep.**

pro·fes·sion·al [prə·fesh′ən·əl] *adj.* Describes people who are paid for what they do: **The New York Liberty is a women's** *professional* **basketball team.**

pro·gram [prō′gram′] *n.* Events or activities organized to help or teach others: **The city has a** *program* **that helps families find homes.** *syn.* plan

re·cite [ri·sīt′] *v.* To say something from memory: **He learned the poem by heart and is ready to** *recite* **it in front of the class.**

rec·ord [rek′ərd] *n.* A listing of the best achievement: **A third grader set the school** *record* **for best attendance.**

re·turn [ri·tûrn′] *v.* **re·turned** To bring or put something back: **Jess** *returned* **the book to the library when he was finished reading it.**

roam [rōm] *v.* To move or travel around with no purpose: **Wild horses** *roam* **the plains.**

se·ri·ous·ly [sir′ē·əs·lē] *adv.* In a thoughtful and honest way: **Brendan was always making jokes, so I was surprised when he spoke** *seriously* **about his poem.**

spe·ci·fic [spi·sif′ik] *adj.* Having a special quality: **I am looking for a** *specific* **type of boot for hiking.**

splin·ter [splin′tər] *n.* **splin·ters** A very thin, sharp bit that breaks off a larger piece of wood, ice, metal, glass, or other material:

splinters

Wear shoes on the deck, or you might get *splinters* **in your feet from the rough wood.**

sta·di·um [stā′dē·əm] *n.* A large structure with rows of seats built around an open field: **At the football** *stadium,* **I sat behind Jenna.**

streak [strēk] *n.* A rapid movement: **Lightning flashed in a** *streak* **across the sky.**

stub·born [stub′ərn] *adj.* Not easily persuaded or convinced: **That** *stubborn* **mule will not move, no matter what I do.**

sum·mon [sum′ən] *v.* **sum·moned** To order a person to come: **The witness was** *summoned* **to appear in court.**

sur·vive [sər·vīv′] *v.* **sur·vived** To live through a difficult time: **The lost hiker** *survived* **the night on the snowy mountain and was rescued in the morning.** *syn.* outlast

tel·e·graph [tel′ə·graf′] *adj.* Having to do with messages sent and received through a machine by using electrical codes: **She went to the *telegraph* office to send her mother a birthday message.**

Fact File

telegraph The first useful telegraph machine was made by Samuel Morse in 1837. It used wires and electricity to send messages. Signals sent as long bursts of electricity were received at the other end as dashes. Signals sent as short bursts were received as dots. Groups of dots and dashes stand for letters and numbers. For example, the letter *e* is just one dot. This code is called Morse code.

tem·per·a·ture [tem′pər·ə·chər *or* tem′prə·chər] *n.* A measurement that tells in degrees how warm or cold something, such as the air, is: **The *temperature* at night was so low that one blanket wasn't enough to keep her warm.**

Word Origins

temperature At first, *temperature* meant "mixture," such as "a temperature of brass and iron together." Later it was used to mean "mild weather," perhaps as a mixture of warm and cool air. The meaning used today probably came from this.

trail [trāl] *n.* A rough path through land where travel is difficult: **The forest *trail* had been made by settlers crossing the mountains.**

trail

train [trān] *v.* **trained** To teach people or animals to do something well by having them repeat the task over and over: **At batting practice, Mr. Lee *trained* us to keep our eyes on the ball.** *syn.* instruct

un·ex·pect·ed [un′ik·spek′tid] *adj.* Surprising; unplanned: **They were happy when their grandparents arrived for an *unexpected* visit.**

van·ish [van′ish] *v.* To go out of sight; to pass from sight: **The sun seemed to *vanish* when clouds covered the sky.** *syn.* disappear

Word Origins

vanish *Vanish* comes from the Latin word *evanescere*, meaning "to become empty" or "to disappear."

wise [wīz] *adj.* Able to understand why things happen in life as they do and to make good decisions based on that understanding: **The *wise* teacher listened to her students and helped them work out an agreement.**

a	add	e	end	o	odd	o͞o	pool	oi	oil	t͟h	this
ā	ace	ē	equal	ō	open	u	up	ou	pout	zh	vision
â	care	i	it	ô	order	û	burn	ng	ring		
ä	palm	ī	ice	o͝o	took	y͞o͞o	fuse	th	thin		

ə = { *a* in *above*, *e* in *sicken*, *i* in *possible*, *o* in *melon*, *u* in *circus* }

Index of Titles

Page numbers in color refer to biographical information.

and Authors

Acknowledgments

For permission to reprint copyrighted material, grateful acknowledgment is made to the following sources:

Arte Público Press - University of Houston: Pepita Talks Twice by Ofelia Dumas Lachtman. Text copyright © 1995 by Ofelia Dumas Lachtman.

Candlewick Press, Inc., Cambridge, MA: "The Talent Show" from *Don't Call Me Beanhead!* by Susan Wojciechowski, cover illustration by Susanna Natti. Text © 1994 by Susan Wojciechowski; cover illustration © 1994 by Susanna Natti.

Children's Television Workshop, New York, NY: From "A Place of Their Own" by Carol Pugliano in *Contact Kids* Magazine, March 1998. Text copyright © 1998 by Children's Television Workshop.

Clarion Books/a Houghton Mifflin Company imprint: Rosie, a Visiting Dog's Story by Stephanie Calmenson, photographs by Justin Sutcliffe. Text copyright © 1994 by Stephanie Calmenson; photographs copyright © 1994 by Justin Sutcliffe.

Tui De Roy: From "Wild Shots, They're My Life" by Tui De Roy in *Ranger Rick* Magazine, August 1996.

Dorling Kindersley Publishing, Inc.: "The Hare and the Tortoise" from *The Lion and the Mouse and Other Aesop's Fables,* retold by Doris Orgel. Text copyright © 2000 by Doris Orgel.

Farrar, Straus & Giroux, Inc.: Turtle Bay by Saviour Pirotta, illustrated by Nilesh Mistry. Text copyright © 1997 by Saviour Pirotta; illustrations copyright © 1997 by Nilesh Mistry.

HarperCollins Publishers: From *Ramona Forever* by Beverly Cleary, cover illustration by Alan Tiegreen. Text copyright © 1984 by Beverly Cleary; cover illustration copyright © 1984 by William Morrow & Company. "The Young Rooster" from *Fables* by Arnold Lobel. Copyright © 1980 by Arnold Lobel.

Highlights for Children, Inc., Columbus, OH: "The Last Case of the I.C. Detective Agency" by Carol M. Harris and cover illustration by Cheryl Kirk Noll from *Highlights for Children* Magazine, January 1996. Text and cover illustration copyright © 1996 by Highlights for Children, Inc.

Holiday House, Inc.: Little Grunt and the Big Egg by Tomie dePaola. Copyright © 1990 by Tomie dePaola.

Alfred A. Knopf Children's Books, a division of Random House, Inc.: "Two Mice" from *In A Circle Long Ago* by Nancy Van Laan. Text copyright © 1995 by Nancy Van Laan.

Lee & Low Books Inc., 95 Madison Ave., New York, NY 10016: Allie's Basketball Dream by Barbara E. Barber, illustrated by Darryl Ligasan. Text copyright © 1996 by Barbara E. Barber; illustrations copyright © 1996 by Darryl Ligasan.

Little, Brown and Company (Inc.): From *Centerfield Ballhawk* by Matt Christopher, cover illustration by Ellen Beier. Text copyright © 1992 by Matthew F. Christopher; cover illustration copyright © 1992 by Ellen Beier.

G. P. Putnam's Sons, an imprint of Penguin Putnam Books for Young Readers, a division of Penguin Putnam Inc.: Officer Buckle and Gloria by Peggy Rathmann. Copyright © 1995 by Peggy Rathmann.

Random House Children's Books, a division of Random House, Inc.: "Gloria, Who Might Be My Best Friend" from *The Stories Julian Tells* by Ann Cameron, cover illustration by Ann Strugnell. Text copyright © 1981 by Ann Cameron; cover illustration copyright © 1981 by Ann Strugnell. Illustrations by Martha Weston from *Nate the Great, San Francisco Detective* by Marjorie Weinman Sharmat and Mitchell Sharmat. New illustrations of Nate the Great, Sludge, Fang, Annie, Rosamond, the Hexes, and Claude by Martha Weston based upon the original drawings by Marc Simont. All other images copyright © 2000 by Martha Weston.

Marian Reiner on behalf of Constance Kling Levy: "The Swimmer" from *A Tree Place and Other Poems* by Constance Levy. Text copyright © 1994 by Constance Kling Levy.

Anne Rockwell: "The Dog and the Wolf" from *The Acorn Tree and Other Folktales,* retold and illustrated by Anne Rockwell. Copyright © 1995 by Anne Rockwell.

Scholastic Inc.: "Balto, the Dog Who Saved Nome" from *Seven True Dog Stories* by Margaret Davidson, cover illustration by Susanne Suba. Text copyright © 1977 by Margaret Davidson; cover illustration copyright by Scholastic Inc.

M.B. & M.E. Sharmat Trust: Nate the Great, San Francisco Detective by Marjorie Weinman Sharmat and Mitchell Sharmat. Text copyright © 2000 by Marjorie Weinman Sharmat and Mitchell Sharmat.

Shen's Books: From *To Swim in Our Own Pond: A Book of Vietnamese Proverbs,* collected and translated by Ngoc-Dung Tran. Text copyright © 1998 by Ngoc-Dung Tran.

Simon & Schuster Books for Young Readers, an imprint of Simon & Schuster Children's Publishing Division: "All My Hats" from *Secrets of a Small Brother* by Richard J. Margolis, cover illustration by Donald Carrick. Text copyright © 1984 by Richard J. Margolis; cover illustration copyright © 1984 by Donald Carrick.

Steck-Vaughn Company: From *Baseball: How To Play the All-Star Way* (Retitled: "Spotlight On Baseball") by Mark Alan Teirstein. Text copyright © 1994 by Steck-Vaughn Company.

Photo Credits

Key: (t)=top; (b)=bottom; (c)=center; (l)=left; (r)=right
Page 37, Dale Higgins; 63, Peter Stone / Black Star; 95(t), courtesy, Marjorie & Mitchell Sharmat; 95(b), Dale Higgins; 97, Bettmann / Corbis; 120, 121, Black Star; 122, Bettmann Archive / Corbis; 123, 124, Duomo; 130, M. Thonig / H. Armstrong Roberts; 131, D. R. Stoecklein / Corbis Stock Market; 132(tl), 132-133, Bill Frakes / TimePix; 134(t), Hulton / Archive Photos; 134(b), Bettmann / Corbis; 135, Corbis; 136-137, Earl Kowall / Corbis; 136, Reuters / Mike Blake / Archive Photos; 137, 138(t), AFP / Corbis; 138(b), Culver Pictures; 139, Tony Duffy / Allsport USA; 140, TimePix; 141(t), AFP / Corbis; 141, Bettmann / Corbis; 142, Sports Illustrated; 143, Al Bello / Allsport USA; 144(t), 144, 145, 146(t), AFP / Corbis; 146-147, Reuters NewMedia Inc. / Corbis; 182(t), The Granger Collection, New York; 182(bl), Allen Prier / AlaskaStock; 182(br), Harry Walker / AlaskaStock; 183(t), Harcourt Photo Library; 183(bl), Jeff Schultz / AlaskaStock; 183(br), David Stoecklein / Corbis Stock Market; 184, 196, 198, UPI / Corbis; 199, Rick Friedman / Black Star; 208-217, 220, Tui de Roy; 245, Suki Coughlin / Styled by Paula McFarland; 246-247, AFP / Corbis; 248, Photo provided courtesy of Black Hills Institute, Hill City, SD, Peter Larson, photographer.; 249, 250, Ira Block / National Geographic Society; 251, Reuters NewMedia Inc./ Corbis; 253, Francois Gohier / Photo Researchers, Inc.; 258-278, Justin Sutcliffe; 298, 299, 321, 349(t), Black Star; 349(b), courtesy, Matt Christopher; 381, Margaret Miller; 385, Jose L. Pelaez / Corbis Stock Market; 435, Ken Kinzie / Harcourt; 436, Richard A. Cooke III / Stone; 438(l), Ed Degginer / Bruce Coleman, Inc.; 438(tr), D.R. Stoecklein / Corbis Stock Market; 438(br), Michael Levine / Index Stock Photography; 439, Harcourt Photo Library; 441, Jeffry W. Myers / Corbis Stock Market.

Illustration Credits

Leland Klanderman, Cover Art; Tungwai Chau, 4-5, 12-13; Tracy Sabin, 6-7, 154-155; Cindy Lindgren, 8-9, 280-281; Ethan Long, 10-11, 151, 327, 406; Steve Björkman, 14-15; Peggy Rathman, 16-37; Tuko Fujisaki, 39; Jill Newton, 42-43; William Low, 44-63; Nancy Davis, 66; Jeff Shelly, 68-69; Martha Weston, 70-95; Dona Turner, 100-101; Darryl Ligasan, 102-121; Mike DiGiorgio, 122-125, 350; Chris Van Dusen, 127, 301; Kurt Nagahori, 148-149; Tamara Petrosino, 156-157; Nilesh Mistry, 158-177; Doug Rugh, 184-199; Vilma Ortiz-Dillon, 200-201; Russ Willms, 206-207; Cathy Bennett, 221; Tony Griego, 224-225; Tomie de Paola, 226-245; Tom Leonard, 246-249; Jackie Snider, 253; Liz Callen, 256-257; Nancy Coffelt, 277; Joe Cepeda, 282-283; Cornelius Van Wright/Ying-Hwa Hu, 284-299; Mercedes McDonald, 304-305; Laura Ovresat, 306-321, 405; Linda Helton, 322-323; Keiko Motoyama, 330-331; Larry Johnson, 332-349, 351; Stacie Peterson, 356-357; Diane Greenseid, 358-381; Robert Casilla, 382-383; Stephen Snider, 388-389; Krystyna Stasiak, 390-403.